WITHDRAWN

I Had That Doll!

A GLORYA HALE BOOK
This 1996 edition is published by Park Lane Press,
a division of Random House Value Publishing, Inc.,
40 Engelhard Avenue, Avenel, New Jersey 07001.

Park Lane Press and its colophon are registered
trademarks of Random House Value Publishing, Inc.

Random House
New York • Toronto • London • Sydney • Auckland
http://www.randomhouse.com/

Design by Kathryn Wolgast Plosica
Editorial supervision by Nina Rosenstein and Carol Kelly Gangi
Production supervision by Roméo Enriquez

Printed and bound in the United States of America

Library of Congress Cataloging-in-Publication Data
I had that doll! / by the Editors of Doll Reader.
p. cm.
ISBN 0-517-20051-1 (hard cover)
1. Dolls—History—20th century. I. Doll Reader.
NK4894.A2I2   1996
688.7'221'0904—dc20

96-17664
CIP

8 7 6 5 4 3 2 1

I Had That Doll!

Special Photography by Rich Beitzel

Text by Carolyn Cook,
Michilinda Kinsey, and
Scott Wood

PARK LANE PRESS

New York · Avenel

Contents

Introduction

In 1904, four-year-old Esta's beloved "Martin doll" was rescued from the burning family home. Almost a century later, this doll is treasured by Esta's great-niece.

DOLLS HAVE ALMOST CERTAINLY EXISTED as long as men, women, and children. It is not difficult to imagine a cave child pretending that a stick, a bone, or a piece of fur was her "baby." We do know that there have been dolls in every society and that practically every known material has at some time been used to make them. Wood, wax, metal, porcelain, plastic, cloth, papier-mâché, celluloid, and dozens of other materials have been fashioned into dolls.

The doll is an emotional extension of the child. It embodies the need for an empathetic attachment. Most women, and some men, often remember the great pleasure a favorite doll gave them during childhood. With a doll, unlike almost any other object, there can be an emotional tie that carries through our lives.

Several years ago, my great-aunt Esta, my grandmother's youngest sister, presented me with her favorite childhood doll. There had been a great age difference between my grandmother and my aunt, and when my grandparents became engaged, my grandfather gave his fiancée's small sister a doll. Aunt Esta called it her "Martin doll," after my grandfather, and she carried it everywhere.

A year or so later, in 1904, my great-grandparents' home caught fire. The family escaped unharmed, but when four-year-old Esta realized her Martin doll was still in the burning house she tried to go back to save it. Realizing her distress, older brothers and sisters did return to the burning house. The Martin doll was the only thing saved, with the exception of a drawer of old hats one enterprising sibling carried out.

When she was in her seventies, Esta gave the cherished doll to me. It has a bisque head with bright blue glass sleep eyes (very much the color of Esta's and my grandmother's eyes) and a gangling wood and composition body. It is a doll that was made for at least forty years—from the 1890s up to the 1930s—by a German firm, Armand Marseille. When she was given to me, the doll had been in the attic for years, but she still wore her original dress, which appeared to be either black or dark gray, and one original red shoe. After several gentle washings, the dress turned out to be a red-and-white plaid, explaining the choice of shoe color.

She was an inexpensive doll in her day. I'm sure young Martin bought it on an impulse, probably at the company store in the sawmill town where he worked. After almost thirty years of collecting dolls, I have many that are much rarer and far more expensive than this one, but if my house ever caught fire, the Martin doll would be rescued before any of the others. After all, she is "family."

This book takes a nostalgic look back at some of the favorite dolls of past generations—dolls that you, your mother, and your grandmother may remember. Included is an ample selection of many of the most popular dolls of each decade of the twentieth century. Some were important because they were such commercial successes: the Kewpies, the Bye-Lo Baby, the Cabbage Patch Kids, and, of course, Barbie. Others are included because they were so new or innovative for their time that they caught the public imagination: Boudoir dolls, Betsy Wetsy, Chatty Cathy and G.I. Joe. Others have a timeless quality and have become household names: Raggedy Ann, Shirley Temple, and Ginny.

Whatever your taste, and whatever your age, this book is for you. Whether you remember your very best doll friend being made of bisque, composition, cloth, or plastic, we hope you find her included. Look through the pages—and hopefully you will exclaim, "I had that doll!"

CAROLYN COOK

A Brief History of Dolls

The earliest type of mass-produced doll made in Germany was of papier-mâché. Her hairstyle dates this doll to around 1840.

This German bisque doll has a jointed composition body and glass sleep eyes.

FOR SEVERAL CENTURIES, the center of the doll-making world was Europe. Prior to 1800, dolls, like everything else, were handmade and one-of-a-kind. Wood and cloth were popular materials for making dolls because they were readily available.

Wooden dolls were carved by craftsmen whose skills ranged from crude to sophisticated. The beauty of these dolls is not always obvious to modern eyes. They often have eyebrows painted in dots that resemble caterpillars crawling across their foreheads, and forklike hands with long thin fingers. Others have carved tiara-like headpieces that attempt to depict the decorative combs tucked into hairstyles popular at the time the dolls were made.

Cloth has been a traditional material for making dolls. Bits of rag and other discards could be easily crafted into a child's toy by a mother or grandmother. Most very old rag dolls have long disappeared, but the comfort of this kind of cuddly doll lives on in such mass-produced twentieth-century descendants as Raggedy Ann and Holly Hobbie.

The beginnings of the mass-produced doll were in Germany shortly after 1800. Toy papier-mâché animals had been made in Thuringia for generations, and pressing the mâché into molds to make dolls' heads was a logical advance. These papier-mâché heads were made for many years and revolutionized the doll industry. Thousands of doll heads could be made from the same mold, and although the dolls' faces were still painted by hand, they could be made relatively fast and inexpensively. Only the head and shoulders were papier-mâché. The bodies were made of kid or cloth and the limbs were usually carved wood. The papier-mâché dolls had molded hairdos that reflected the popular styles of the day. Many of them are reminiscent of the pictures of young Queen Victoria, with wings of hair sweeping down in front of their ears.

Although dolls were produced in such other materials as wax, by the mid nineteenth century porcelain became the material of choice for dolls' heads. Like papier-mâché, it could be molded and mass-produced. The two basic types of porcelain dolls were made of china or bisque.

The china heads resemble the papier-mâché dolls' heads; they usually have molded hairstyles and painted features. They were made of glazed porcelain, so they have a shiny surface, just like plates, teacups, or other china items. They were especially popular between 1840 and 1870, but continued to be manufactured through the first decades of the twentieth century. China heads, and sometimes matching china limbs, were often put on bodies of cloth or kid. Complete dolls could be purchased, but the dolls' heads could be bought separately. It was not unusual to buy a doll's head and sew a body for it at home, making the toy much less expensive. The wholesale cost of a china head might range from five cents to one dollar and twenty-five cents.

By the last quarter of the nineteenth century, unglazed porcelain dolls' heads, called bisque or bisquit, had become popular. The matte finish and fine texture of these heads resembled the appearance of skin far more than shiny china. At first, the bisque heads were usually put on kid bodies, but when jointed bodies of composition were invented, they became the rage. The ball-jointed bodies allowed the dolls to be seated and posed in realistic postures. Other innovations with the bisque heads made the dolls more "human." They were given wigs of mohair, lambswool, or even human hair. Glass eyes were inset for realism. Soon sleep eyes, which closed when the doll was laid down, were invented. Finally, open mouths showing tiny pearly teeth were made. Although these dolls were considered realistic by the Victorians, today they look very idealized with their creamy, perfect bisque "skin," huge luminous eyes, heavy eyebrows, and exuberantly frilled and ruffled costumes.

Germany and France were giants in the manufacture of bisque-headed dolls. By the end of the nineteenth century, doll

With set glass "paperweight" eyes, bisque heads, and ball-jointed composition bodies, these three French bisque bébé's date from the 1890s.

making was an enormous industry and dolls were exported all over the world. Millions of dolls were made each year and all the major department stores in the United States and Europe sent buyers or had offices in the Sonneberg area of Thuringia.

Germany had a lengthy tradition of toymaking, and, especially in the Thuringian area, families had long been exploited as cheap labor. Much of the work was done in homes as a cottage industry. Children as well as adults stuffed bodies, pressed out dolls' limbs in papier-mâché, or did similar piecework. Often the working conditions were bad, with entire families working in a single unventilated room.

Factory conditions were perhaps a bit better. There, workers specialized in painting the eyebrows and eyelashes, painting mouths, cutting out eye sockets, or setting glass eyes. Each worker would perform her specialty and then pass the head or the body to the next worker.

The French doll industry was aimed at the affluent customer. French dolls were dressed in beautiful clothing and were packaged to appeal to the prosperous buyer. In the 1870s and 1880s, lovely lady dolls were made with costumes and accessories that were sold separately, much like the modern Barbie industry. The lady dolls, called Parisiennes, could be outfitted in a variety of high-style gowns, capes, gloves, hats, and shoes. They also had such accessories as furniture, dishes, toiletries, and jewelry—all the little luxuries real ladies of fashion required.

A few adventuresome doll makers, especially in France, experimented with dolls that moved with clockwork mechanisms. Dolls were created that could play musical instruments, fan themselves, dance, do magic tricks, and accomplish various other "real" activities. These automata were quite expensive and intended more for adult entertainment than as toys for children.

Later in the century, the French doll makers invented the *bébé*—a bisque-headed little-girl doll that had an idealized face with large luminous eyes and elegant costumes. Until the end of the nineteenth century, when Kate Greenaway styles became popular, children were dressed as miniature adults as soon as they began to walk. Their dolls were dressed the same way.

For some years, the French contracted with manufacturers in Germany to make bisque dolls' heads which would be put on bodies in France, costumed there, and marketed as "French" dolls. Since the competition between the doll makers in the two countries was so intense, it is not surprising that the excellent German businessmen decided it would be to their advantage to create similar dolls and market them themselves. They had the mass-marketing abilities to be highly competitive in price. It was they who brought the bisque-headed doll into the price range of middle-class families, few of whom could afford a French *bébé*. In 1895 the John Wanamaker department store, in New York City, advertised a thirteen-inch French doll with a bisque head and a composition body for thirteen dollars. In the same ad, German bisque-headed dolls (sizes not mentioned) ranged in price from fifty cents to nine dollars.

In the final years of the nineteenth century, Germany and France were battling for the advantage in world trade for the doll market. By 1899, however, the French doll manufacturers realized that as separate entities they could no longer compete with the German doll makers, so they joined forces in a syndicate. In 1910, the innovative idea of making dolls resemble real children rather than idealized adults improved business in Germany and France. Called character dolls, these new dolls had faces that displayed real emotions: they laughed, they cried, or they frowned. Baby dolls were made, too. These realistic babies would not have been acceptable toys for Victorian children, but standards were rapidly changing for this new century. Clever manufacturers made bodies with bent limbs that not only looked like the arms and legs of real babies, but were simpler and cheaper to manufacture than the limbs made in several pieces that required ball joints.

In addition to the bisque dolls being imported from Europe, cloth dolls were widely available to American children.

By the turn of the century, sewing machines had become a fixture in many American homes. Consequently, dolls printed in color on fabric that could be bought by the yard became extremely popular. The Arnold Print Works of North Adams, Massachusetts, printed material with dolls that were intended to be cut out, sewed, and then stuffed at home.

In 1892, Arnold Print Works introduced the Brownies, based on the characters created by Palmer Cox, a Canadian illustrator. The Brownies first appeared in *Saint Nicholas*, the influential children's magazine. Drawn from the tales of sprites, gnomes, and brownies spun by Cox's Scottish ancestors, the Brownies quickly became the biggest hit of the turn of the century. The first book of the Brownies, *The Brownies, Their Book*, was published in 1887 and from then until the second decade of the twentieth century it seemed as if the Brownies—whose roster had increased to about fifty characters—were everywhere.

They were paper dolls, and appeared on souvenir cups, spoons, playing cards, puzzles, and prints. They appeared in advertisements for everything from Estey Organs to the Eastman Kodak Company's Brownie camera. Some say the camera was named after the creatures. The Brownies were also replicated in porcelain, terra-cotta, and, most popular, in cloth.

A yard of Brownies cost about twenty cents, and hundreds of thousands of yards were sold. A dozen characters, including Chinaman, Dude, Highlander, Indian, John Bull, Uncle Sam, and Policeman, were printed on the fabric. "These funny little fellows have been produced in the most attractive coloring on cloth," announced an Arnold's advertisement. "There are twelve in number and all come in one yard, easily cut out, sewed together, then stuffed with cotton, bran, or sawdust. About seven inches in length, they can be bent into any position."

Over the years, the cloth Brownies have been reproduced many times by many manufacturers. It is possible that they are still selling somewhere today. What adventures they would have in the late twentieth century!

This Brownie doll, ready to stitch and stuff, was produced on cloth by the Cocheco Manufacturing Company, a competitor of Arnold. For just ten cents, by mail, a child could order this big-eyed, bowlegged fellow, who was "full of fun," according to the advertisement.

1910–1919

THE SECOND DECADE OF THE TWENTIETH CENTURY brought changes that would have been unimaginable a few years before. In 1913, Henry Ford put the first assembly line in operation. This new efficiency in mass-production would become the foundation for the manufacturing of nearly all products. Certainly the manufacture of dolls would change drastically.

The attitude toward children, and children's toys and play, was also changing. Up until the eighteenth century the concept of childhood was of no concern. Before then, children were considered to be miniature adults and therefore not deserving of any kind of special treatment. The Montessori method, first used in the United States early in the twentieth century, was a strong influence in teaching that children had specific requirements.

The opinion that children's dolls should be more realistic was quite revolutionary. One of the first to create realistic dolls was Käthe Kruse, a housewife. She became a doll maker in 1900 after the birth of her second child prompted her three-year-old daughter to request a child of her own—"like her mother had"—for Christmas. Käthe Kruse made dolls that little children could "mother" and founded a company that is still thriving.

In 1908, Marion Kaulitz organized a group of German artists to make dolls with individualistic faces, as opposed to the insipid "dolly" faces of many of the then popular bisque dolls. An exhibition of these dolls was held at a department store in Munich and later in Paris. These art dolls had painted faces and were not mass-produced; but they were priced competitively with other dolls, and they may have influenced the

widespread popularity of the bisque character dolls that hit the market about 1910.

The assassination of Archduke Ferdinand and his wife in Sarajevo was the catalyst for World War I. The war brought developments in technology that ultimately affected commodities other than weapons. Since Germany was now the enemy, there was a reluctance in the United States to buy merchandise produced there. Suddenly the need for American-made products was realized in the toy industry. Other than those from Schoenhut and Ideal, and several small companies run by such ladies as Ella Smith, Martha Chase, Julia Beecher, and Emma Adams, few dolls were manufactured on this side of the Atlantic.

Because of the shortage of dolls during the war, some companies jumped into the breach and made dolls for a short time. One such company was the Fulper Pottery Company in Flemington, New Jersey, which was known for kitchen tableware. During the war years they made dolls' heads. After the war they returned to making pottery.

Other new doll companies were born. Three of the best-known names are Effanbee, begun in 1912 and still in existence; the Ideal company, launched in 1907 and best known for Shirley Temple dolls in the 1930s; and the Averill Manufacturing Company, started in 1915. Composition became a favorite doll-making material about 1912, and most of the American companies made dolls from this new substance. This was truly the beginning of the American doll industry.

The Campbell Kids

THE CAMPBELL KIDS GOT THEIR START on trolley cars in Philadelphia. The creation of Grace G. Drayton, an illustrator, these roly-poly youngsters first appeared about 1904 in streetcar advertisements for condensed soup. When the ads began to run in such magazines as *Ladies Home Journal* they caught the eyes of mothers and daughters all over the country. About five years later, Drayton, in response to public demand, designed the first Campbell Kids doll.

From the start, the Kids were almost unbearably cute with their chubby cheeks, very slightly flattened noses, thick legs, and dimpled knees. Their eyes looked mischievously to the side, as if they had just eaten something considerably sweeter and more fattening than chicken noodle soup.

The first Kids were made by E. I. Horsman in 1910 and had unbreakable composition heads and cloth bodies. They were androgynous and came in a variety of sizes. A ten-inch Campbell Junior, shown in a 1914 Sears, Roebuck catalog, came dressed as a girl in a flowered dress, but when the dress was removed "she" became a boy wearing a checked romper suit.

Early Campbell Kids dolls are often confused with Bobby Blake and Dolly Drake, two other characters created by Drayton and made as dolls about the same time. Bobby and Dolly are now only collectibles, occasionally mentioned in articles in antiques and collectors' publications.

The Campbell Kids, however, play on and on. They almost disappeared during the Great Depression, but reappeared in the 1940s in advertisements supporting the war effort with the slogan "Better Soups for Victory."

From 1947 to 1950, Sears, Roebuck catalogs offered twelve-and-a-half-inch

Twelve inches tall, this pair of adorable composition Campbell Kids was made by E. I. Horsman.

Campbell Kids with molded hair. The boy wore shorts with suspenders and a striped shirt. One of the girls was dressed in a matching outfit; the other wore a checked dress. These were the last of the composition Kids. Beginning in 1950 they were made of vinyl.

One of the early Campbell Kids, this charming eleven-inch tot was made by Horsman. The head is composition, but the cloth body is soft and cuddly.

As with many other toys that brighten our collective memory, it was television that really made the Campbell Kids famous as characters and as dolls. They were streamlined for animated Campbell's soup commercials, but all in all they remained pretty much the same. By 1954 more than thirty manufacturers were licensed to produce Campbell Kids merchandise, including, of course, dolls.

When Campbell was sponsoring *Lassie* on television, children all over America watched the show while absently clutching one of Horsman's Campbell Kids dressed as a chef. Ideal Novelty and Toy Company also made a pair of Campbell Kids dressed as chefs, with hard-plastic bodies and vinyl heads that could swivel. These dolls had "magic skin," so called because the heads had flexibility and were smooth to the touch. Better yet, when you squeezed one (or your brother accidentally sat on it) the doll cooed.

Since the 1950s, Campbell Kids have been manufactured in various materials, sizes, and costumes. In 1994, to celebrate Campbell's 125th anniversary, the company packaged the dolls in large soup cans. About the same time, a small cloth doll appeared in toy stores.

Those Campbell Kids don't seem to have aged a day since 1904. Eternally cherubic and wholesome, they are still humming about the quality of a bowl of you-know-what.

The Kewpies

Scootles

Rose O'Neill and Joseph Kallus collaborated on another doll whose popularity, although nothing like that of the Kewpies, did make a mark and is still a favorite among collectors. He is androgynous, like the Kewpies, but he looks like a male—and his name is Scootles. According to the story, he was a tourist, scooting all over the world.

These paper dolls, called Kewpie Kutouts, appeared in a 1913 issue of **Woman's Home Companion**. *These Kewpies display an adorable pair of wings. The instructions read: "Cut out both the back and the front view of the Kewp Who Wears His Overshoes and paste the two views very neatly together. Put a light weight on them for a few minutes to keep them flat and even. Then bend the red base forward for the Kewp to stand up straight on."*

ROSE O'NEILL, AN ARTIST, claimed that the idea of Kewpies came to her in a dream. The rest is history. These chubby, sexless, elfin cherubs were, according to O'Neill, modeled on her baby brother. A Kewpie, she said, is the baby form of Cupid. Its purpose is to do good deeds in a humorous way, instilling humans with love and brightening their existence with laughter.

The Kewpies began as decorations for love stories published in *Ladies Home Journal*. The magazine's editor suggested that O'Neill tighten up the drawings, develop the characters, and add stories in verse for young readers. The first Kewpie story appeared in 1909. It was titled "The Kewpies and the Airplane" and showed the little creatures investigating the new mechanical wonder of the age. More stories followed. Their popularity exploded. Children enchanted by the verses and the drawings wrote in asking if there was a Kewpie they could actually hold.

O'Neill sculpted the first Kewpie herself. She visited doll factories throughout the United States and Europe before selecting a manufacturer in Germany. George Borgfeldt secured the rights to distribute Kewpies in America and, in a nice bit of well-timed publicity, *Woman's Home Companion* carried a story entitled "How the Kewpies Turned Into Dolls."

The little Kewpies were big. The Kewpie craze became so big that thirty German factories were kept busy manufacturing the dolls. By 1913, about five million Kewpies had been sold.

World War I put an end to the German connection. But even warfare didn't keep the Kewpies out of the stores. Factories in Japan, many unauthorized by O'Neill, took advantage of the opportunity and launched thousands

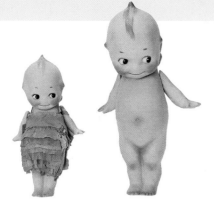

Kewpies were made in a variety of sizes. They were androgynous and ageless, until they were dressed.

The Kewpies and Brother Dan
By Rose O'Neill

This story, featuring the Kewpies, appeared in a 1913 issue of **Woman's Home Companion.**

of Kewpies into the American market.

After the war ended, O'Neill delegated the manufacture of her Kewpies to Joseph Kallus, a young sculptor. Kallus, with O'Neill's permission, had helped design Kewpie figurines for German manufacturers when he was only seventeen years old. In 1916 he had founded the Rex Doll Company to produce composition Kewpies when supplies from overseas were halted during the war. Later, Kallus's Kewpies were plastic, then vinyl. Kallus kept Kewpies alive until the early 1980s.

Over the years numerous manufacturers were licensed to produce Kewpies. You might have owned a hard-plastic, fully jointed Kewpie with sleep eyes that was produced by the Effanbee Doll Company. Or perhaps in the late 1960s you had a Kewpie made by Knickerbocker or by Milton Bradley.

The International Rose O'Neill Club, founded in the late 1960s, holds a Kewpiesta—a four-day Kewpie collectors' convention and festival—every April at Bonniebrook, O'Neill's Missouri home.

During World War I, soldiers marched off to the hell of the trenches with tiny Kewpies in their pockets. The dolls were reminders of loved ones and were good-luck tokens. Judging from the comments of collectors, people still keep Kewpies around for pretty much the same reasons. Now almost a century old, Kewpies are still doing their job. They're making people happy.

Raggedy Ann

RAGGEDY ANN IS ARGUABLY THE MOST BELOVED American doll of the twentieth century. She certainly isn't glamorous. She doesn't even have a wardrobe. But it's almost impossible not to hug Raggedy Ann, and perhaps that is the reason the sales of the dolls have been astronomical.

Raggedy Ann's origin is shrouded in legend. Some stories say that Johnny Gruelle, an artist and the doll's creator, found his mother's old doll in the attic, dusted off the years, painted a new face over the old faded one, and gave the doll to his daughter Marcella.

John B. Gruelle, who was born in Illinois on Christmas Eve, 1880, was an astute businessman and registered Raggedy Ann as a trademark as early as 1915. The doll's name was culled from two characters—The Raggedy Man and Little Orphant Annie—about whom poems were written by James Whitcomb Riley, the famous Hoosier poet and a family friend.

In 1916, Marcella died at the age of fourteen. Gruelle's book, *Raggedy Ann Stories*, inspired by her devotion to the new old doll, was published two years later. From the start, children (and their parents) wanted a Raggedy Ann of their own. Reportedly, the first dolls were made by members of the Gruelle family, working out of a corner of a friend's shirt factory. Eventually, demand overran production and commercial mass-production of the doll began.

P. V. Volland, the publisher of the book, is usually cited as the first commercial company to manufacture Raggedy Ann. Whether Volland actually made the dolls or contracted with a manufacturer is a question about which collectors continue to squabble.

The early Raggedy Anns have brownish hair rather than the red most people recognize. They might have been made in a variety of sizes, but sixteen inches tall seems to have been common. Collectors and Raggedy Ann aficionados say that the earliest dolls—those made by the family—had

This fifteen-inch Raggedy Ann was made by Knickerbocker Toy Company. A label sewn on her apron says: "Johnny Gruelle's own Raggedy Ann doll."

candy hearts with "I Love You" printed on them, like the doll heroine of the book. Mothers began to complain that children cut the hearts out and ate them. Consequently, hearts made of other materials, like stiff cardboard and wood, were used.

In 1920, Raggedy Ann's brother, Andy, entered the Raggedy mythology with the publication of Gruelle's *Raggedy Andy Stories.*

The Raggedy dolls' popularity was not relegated to the nursery. No one, of any age, could resist the Raggedys. There were Raggedy Ann and Andy greeting cards, games, a musical based on the stories and characters, and a fox-trot (punctuated by a lot of hugging) called the Raggedy Ann.

Volland made the dolls until 1934, when the company succumbed to the Great Depression. Another company, Molly-'es, took advantage of the lull in production and began producing its own Raggedy Ann and Andy dolls. Gruelle fought for the right to his own creations, and after more than two years in court (while Molly-'es continued to produce the dolls) Gruelle won. The dolls manufactured by Molly-'es, regardless of their unauthorized nature, are considered by collectors to be well made and properly dressed.

After Gruelle's legal victory, Georgene Novelties, Inc., a company established by Georgene Averill, the well-known doll designer, took over for the next twenty-five years. The dolls made by Georgene Novelties ranged in height from twelve to more than thirty inches. During the 1940s, McCall's Pattern Company was licensed to market do-it-yourself patterns for Raggedy Ann and Andy, resulting in an abundance of homemade Raggedys during the late 1940s and 1950s. Since the 1960s, Knickerbocker Toy Company, Applause Toy Company, and Hasbro have all produced Raggedy dolls, ensuring that after all these years Raggedy Ann and Andy will continue to delight children with their sunniness, adventures, and happy endings.

Made in 1951 by Georgene Novelties, this Raggedy Ann is sixteen inches tall.

Topsy-Turvy

TOPSY-TURVY DOLLS, ESPECIALLY THE RAG DOLLS, were commercially produced and handmade for many decades. Just about everyone of a certain age remembers Topsy-Turvy dolls. Owning one was like having two, since each doll had two heads and torsos, one at each end, and no legs. While one head was upright and facing you, a skirt hid the other head, which was below, upside down.

Topsy-Turvy dolls were made of composition, celluloid, even ceramic. If your Topsy-Turvy was handed down in the family for a couple of generations, it might bear the date 1901, when Albert Bruckner, who lived in New Jersey and made rag dolls, was awarded a patent for inventing a way to mount painted, stiffened fabric faces on his dolls. Topsy-Turvy was one kind of doll in his line. The most popular of these two-headed creatures, however, were made of cloth.

You might have received your Topsy-Turvy as a project. That is, your doll might have been a Dolly Double, a cutout rag doll. All that was needed to make the doll were basic sewing tools and thread. And, perhaps, an adult to do the sewing.

Judging from the recollections of those who remember these dolls, most of the Topsy-Turvy dolls had one white doll and one African-American mirror image. Some of the dolls wore reversible dresses. The white doll, for example, wore a blue-checked country dress with a white apron and a delicate bonnet. The black doll wore a red-and-white-checked dress and a white apron with a kerchief around her head like a turban.

Another popular variation of Topsy-Turvy had one head that was smiling, the other crying. Yet another kind of cutout reversible doll, produced around the first decade of the twentieth century, had one head wearing a hat, the other head bare. Teddy Turnover was also popu-

This is a typical Topsy-Turvy doll—one head is awake, the other is sleeping. The bonnets and dresses of the dolls are different, truly creating two dolls in one.

lar in the same period. One doll was a reasonably realistic representation of a young lady, or a young man, while at the other end there was a bear. Or you might have owned a doll with Red Riding Hood at one end and the wolf at the other, Snow White combined with the witch, or the Raggedy Ann and Andy pair.

Snow White, with the Seven Dwarfs surrounding her, is an unusual modern Topsy-Turvy. The other head is that of the cruel stepmother disguised as the kindly old woman who tempts Snow White with a poisoned apple.

Mama Dolls

MAMA DOLLS ARE SO CALLED because when you tip one of these dolls toward you while rocking her, or give her a big hug, she says "Mama." The early Mama dolls had composition heads, partially composition limbs, and huggable cloth bodies. They ranged in size from ten to twenty-seven inches, and in price from ninety-eight cents to twenty dollars. These dolls were advertised as "almost unbreakable." They were made to be played with.

Effanbee produced the first Mama dolls in 1918. Two years later, the doll could also say "Papa." She was advertised as the "doll with the human voice." There were many names for Mama dolls, and each year there were new ones, including Trottie Trulife in 1921, Dolly Dumpling the following year, and Beach Baby, Nancy Ann, and Honeybunch in 1923.

One Mama doll that achieved special fame was Rosemary. Keeping track of the Mama dolls is a bit difficult because almost all the dolls from the mid-1920s until about 1930, although tagged with such names as Lovey Mary, Mary Lou, Naughty Eyes, and Mary Louise, are marked "Rosemary" on the back of the neck. In time the Rosemary Mama dolls became slenderer and appeared slightly older.

Made by Georgene Averill, this baby doll who says "Mama" has a composition head and limbs and a cloth body.

Rosemary, at least during her early years, had blue eyes with real eyelashes, healthy-hued cheeks, and a little rosebud mouth with tiny teeth and a velvet tongue. Each doll wore an organdy dress, in one of a variety of colors, and a matching bonnet. Around her neck hung a golden chain with a heart-shaped pendant. The heart was inscribed with the company's name. A booklet titled *The Proper Doll for My Child's Age* came with the doll. The booklet gave advice on how playing with the doll could build character.

Your Mama doll, or your mother's, was probably bought at Montgomery Ward or through that company's catalog. The "Most Life-Like Baby Doll in America," exclaimed the copy in a 1921 catalog. "Looks and talks almost like a real baby—and is just the right size too." Several years later, an advertisement for the "twenty-five-inch Ma-ma Baby to Cuddle and Love" described "a cuddly, lovable Baby Doll, just learning to walk and say, 'ma-ma.' She comes to her new mama in a crisp organdy dress and bonnet. With undergarment, socks and slippers you can take off."

Rosemary was the best-known of the Mama dolls. This is one of the earliest. She was made by Effanbee about 1918 and is dressed in her original clothes.

Later in that decade, when the Mama dolls had "Slender, Graceful Bodies," they were advertised in the Montgomery Ward catalog as Effanbee's most beautiful dolls. Rosemary, like most Mama dolls of this time, came with a set of six of her photographs. Rosemary's sister, Mary Sue, had the "latest ringlet bob." Both dolls had stitched wigs of human hair and both would dance or walk with you if you led. You could also seat Rosemary or her sister in a doll carriage with woven fiber reed sides and hood, artillery rubber tire wheels, and corduroy upholstery.

The Mama dolls, as was explained in an ad in the December 1924 issue of *Good Housekeeping*, were the dolls children themselves would choose. They were what a baby doll was supposed to be. And more than seventy years later, despite the introduction of a variety of new designs and materials, the Mama doll, with her universal appeal, has really needed no improvement.

Schoenhut Dolls

DOROTHY SCHOENHUT WANTED A DOLL that her little brother Norman couldn't break. He had already destroyed three of her dolls with lovely bisque heads. Dorothy's father, Gustav Adolph, stepped in. He was the son of Albert Schoenhut, the renowned German-born toy maker. He offered his daughter a new sample doll from the family factory in Philadelphia, Pennsylvania. This wooden doll, he assured her, could withstand even her little brother.

The little brother expressed some doubt. The doll had been dropped from the fifth floor of the factory and received nothing more than a dent on the nose, replied Gustav. Norman, ever keen on quality control, grabbed the doll, ran upstairs, and threw it out a second-story window. What happened next wasn't recorded. But it is safe to assume that the doll survived.

Few early American doll makers reached such heights as the A. Schoenhut Company. Beginning in 1911 Schoenhut dolls had a realistic and individual charm that had been characteristic only of the German and French bisque dolls. In addition, Schoenhut wooden dolls were made to take hard play, even to withstand little brothers. And Schoenhut dolls were flexible and could be put in realistic positions. Photographs in the 1911 *Playthings* magazine, for example, show the dolls standing on one leg, frozen in realistic gestures, dancing, and sitting together as if they were in the middle of a casual conversation.

The early dolls, both girls and boys with either carved or wigged hair, still draw attention and admiration at antiques shows, in private collections, and in museums. Each doll is a unique character. The faces showed as much variation as you see in an entire school.

The early Schoenhut dolls reached their zenith in 1915 with Miss Dolly. She was heralded as the "All-Wood Perfection Art Doll" who could do everything but talk. "No, Miss Dolly is not a real girl, but you can hardly tell the difference," claimed one advertisement. An exaggeration, perhaps, but Miss Dolly was remarkable nevertheless. She had a round face, full cheeks, and a mouth that appeared to be open, revealing four baby teeth. She had pale peach skin and rosy cheeks. Her hair changed with the fashions. And like all good Schoenhuts, she was very flexible. Miss Dolly was a favorite, in all her variations, until 1924.

Schoenhut also made infant dolls. The first babies were named either Tootsie Wootsie or Schnickel-Fritz. They had round faces, smiling painted eyes, and open mouths. There was a choice of hair that was molded or wigged, and either Natural Arms and Legs— that is, baby-like curved limbs—or limbs that were fully jointed. Some of the infants were toddlers, real doll toddlers, another Schoenhut innovation.

The Schoenhut Walkable Doll came out in 1919. The device that enabled the doll to walk earned one of many patents for Schoenhut. The arms of the doll were slightly curved, outstretching so she could be led. As the doll was eased into a step, a drag on her foot allowed the leg to extend. As the doll was shifted to her other foot, that leg moved forward, making it possible for her to take a step. This doll was "not mechanical," stated advertisements. Schoenhut made only toys the child could empower with life. The artisans at Schoenhut were continually experimenting with new kinds of joints, new types of eyes, and different wigging. They even took special orders for dolls that looked like important people of the day. Many of these were commissioned for special occasions.

During the years Schoenhut was producing its dolls, the company also manufactured hundreds of different kinds of toys, from building blocks to toy musical instruments to its celebrated circus sets. Unfortunately, the company did not survive the Great Depression. In 1964 the old Schoenhut factory was razed. Appropriately, an elementary school was built on the site.

The jointing of the wooden Schoenhut dolls allowed them to be posed realistically. The little doll on the left is sixteen inches tall. Her friend is five inches taller.

27

1920–1929

THE AMERICAN DOLL INDUSTRY may have been born during World War I, but it was in the 1920s that it grew into a thriving business. A period of unrest and change, the twenties was a time of extremes. Although the conservatives stood for prohibition and isolationism, the lasting impression of the roaring twenties is excess. Speakeasies, gangsters, and flappers, people who colorfully flouted the establishment, are today associated with this period.

In the twenties it became a fad to use dolls as decorations. Adult women bought "bed dolls" or "boudoir dolls" to add a spot of color where today a decorative pillow might be used. The boudoir dolls were long-limbed and usually dressed in colorful flapper outfits. They were made of fabric, sometimes with composition heads, and often had heavy seductive makeup and occasionally "smoked" cigarettes! Artistically draped on a bed, or on another piece of furniture, perhaps they mirrored in a small way the woman's own assertion of independence. After all, it was in the twenties that restrictive clothing (especially corsets and stays) became a thing of the past for many women. Those who had joined the work force during the war had to wear more comfortable clothing for many jobs. Afterward, the decadent look was in: skirts rose, necklines plunged, and women bobbed their hair. Beads, fringes, and bows were the height of fashion.

Dolls were still being imported from Europe. One of the most popular dolls to be made in Germany, the Bye-Lo Baby, was designed by Grace Storey Putnam, an American artist. Cloth dolls, especially those made of felt, were extremely popular. The epitome of the felt dolls were those made in Turin, Italy, by Madame Elena Scavini, and marketed under her nickname Lenci.

Women who started their own companies accounted for a sizable portion of the new growth in the American doll industry. Although launching a doll company required the same entrepreneurial drive and business expertise as any other enterprise, it is perhaps because the products were associated with females of all ages that women like Madame Beatrice Alexander, Georgene Averill, and Mary Hoyer were able to compete successfully in the male-dominated business world. The costuming of the dolls was of utmost importance to these women. Madame Alexander and Mary Hoyer were really fashion designers on a miniature scale. They bought dolls or hired sculptors to create them. Georgene Averill, however, actually designed the dolls that were sold under her name.

Baby Dolls

Bye-Lo Baby

GRACE STOREY PUTNAM, an art teacher in California, wanted to create a realistic baby doll. To find just the right model she went to hospitals in the Los Angeles area. Finally, she found an infant that embodied her vision. The child was only three days old, born in a small Salvation Army hospital.

The Bye-Lo Baby was the first truly realistic baby doll. Its face was modeled after a three-day-old infant's.

Considering that almost all other baby dolls of the day were impossibly idealistic, the Bye-Lo Baby was revolutionary; it was remarkably realistic. The face looks slightly squished. The head is not perfectly round. The eyes seem to be squinting. There are even fat rolls on the neck. The cloth body is rather froglike, which makes the baby realistically ungainly, yet cuddly to little girls all over the country.

Naturally, a concept so innovative (and ultimately so successful) was rejected by numerous manufacturers. When the baby was finally "born" in 1923, it quickly became so popular that the manufacturer and distributor, George Borgfeldt, couldn't make enough of them to meet the demand. At Christmas, mothers and daughters stood in block-long lines hoping for an opportunity to buy the doll. Retailers called it "The Million Dollar Baby."

Originally, the baby's head was porcelain, made in Germany. At first, the body was composition, but it was changed to cloth early on. The dolls were eventually made with celluloid, rubber, composition, and wooden (made by Schoenhut) heads. Bye-Lo Baby's dress was almost always white batiste with lace trimming down the front.

The success of the Bye-Lo Baby inspired scores of imitators. None, however, made such a splash—or are as cherished by collectors—as "The Million Dollar Baby."

My Dream Baby

ALTHOUGH MY DREAM BABY WAS CREATED solely to cash in on the popularity of The Million Dollar Baby, few turned away from it. Like the famous Bye-Lo Baby, My Dream Baby looked like a newborn.

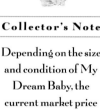

First distributed in 1924 by the Arranbee Doll Company, My Dream Baby had a bisque head made by Armand Marseille, the famous German producer of porcelain and bisque dolls' heads. The head was connected to a composition body by flange or socket neck joints. The baby had either rubber or composition hands. Its eyes, which opened and closed, were made of glass. There was a choice of three sizes. The smallest cost one dollar and twenty-five cents, a good price for a dear baby, even if it was made to cash in on the million-dollar rage of the day.

*My Dream Baby,
a Bye-Lo Baby
copy, came in three
sizes. These two
are the largest and
the smallest.*

Tynie Baby

TYNIE BABY WAS ONE OF THE MANY BYE-LO look-alikes created in the 1920s; nevertheless she deserves a nod of recognition of her own.

Tynie Baby was made in Germany and was distributed by E. I. Horsman of New York City. This baby, designed by Bernard Lipfert, had a round, somewhat idealized face. It was not quite as realistic as the famous Bye-Lo.

Tynie Baby had either a bisque or a composition head and a soft cloth body. A voice box was in the stomach, and when pressed (with a sort of loving Heimlich maneuver) the baby made a crying sound. Tynie Baby came in sizes from eleven to twenty inches.

She was dressed in a white cotton gown trimmed in eyelet lace. Underneath was a white cotton slip. (Layettes for Tynie Baby were available.) Affixed to the gown, just so you'd know for sure, was a pin that read HORSMAN'S TYNIE (sometimes spelled Tinie) BABY.

*Tynie Baby was an
adorable, although not
very realistic, baby doll.*

Baby Peggy

A VETERAN OF A HUNDRED AND FIFTY SHORT COMEDIES and three feature-length films by the age of five, Baby Peggy was cute yet not cloying. She and her male counterpart, Jackie Coogan, were the biggest little stars of the 1920s.

Some of the credit for Baby Peggy's celebrity must be laid at the feet of Sol Lesser, the producer of several of Peggy's films, including *Captain January* and *Helen's Babies.* Lesser, a hard-driving publicist, who probably invented the "personal appearance," signed up the doll manufacturer Louis Amberg & Son to produce a Baby Peggy doll. The doll, which had a bisque head and composition body, was one of innumerable Baby Peggy products that appeared on store shelves during the mid-1920s, most of them to celebrate the child star's fifth birthday. There were Baby Peggy dresses, hats, handbags, jewelry, writing paper, even canned vegetables and fruit.

One Baby Peggy doll was all-bisque and had jointed limbs. She was only about four inches tall and had painted hair, eyes, socks, and shoes. There was also a six-inch bisque Baby Peggy. The most popular Baby Peggy doll, the one that was actually played with, was composition with a relatively huggable cloth body and painted brown hair and eyes. The doll's wide, chubby face was not as cute as that of the little actress, but she was a Baby Peggy doll and at twenty inches was just the right size for a child to carry everywhere. This doll sold for two dollars and fifty cents at Gimbels department store in New York.

On her fifth birthday, Baby Peggy herself was escorted by police to Gimbels to spark sales and meet her fans. From there she went on to F.A.O. Schwarz, then to the New York Foundling Home and a couple of children's hospitals. She made a brief stop to say a few words over the mysterious new medium called radio, then went to Bryant Park where she, a five year old, reviewed a formation of New York City policemen. To top it all off, that night Baby Peggy was hatched out of a gigantic golden egg on the

Baby Peggy was one of the first celebrity dolls. This version was all bisque and only two and a half inches tall.

Jackie Coogan

The years have not diminished the incandescence of Charlie Chaplin's first feature film, *The Kid*. Upon the release of the movie in 1921, Jackie Coogan, who played The Kid, was an instant and nearly worldwide celebrity. Almost immediately his face appeared in newspapers and on magazine covers. Soon afterward, that great face was licensed to sell myriad products, including clothes, figurines, crayons, playing cards, chewing gum, and a doll made by E. I. Horsman and Aetna Doll Company. A button on the doll's shirt identified him as Jackie Coogan Kid.

This kid was fourteen inches tall and had a composition head, shoulder plate, arms, and hands. The body was cloth and jointed. His eyes were painted, as was his hair, molded in the unkempt mop of the movie's hero. He wore a blue or brown turtleneck shirt; tan, dark green, or gray overalls; brown oilcloth slip-on shoes; and a black-and-white-checked hat that was at least one size too big and cocked at a jaunty angle. Just like the movie star. More than two hundred thousand Jackie Coogan dolls were sold.

stage of New York's huge Hippodrome Theater, where Victor Herbert's holiday opera *Toyland* was being performed.

Baby Peggy, whose real name was Diana Serra, toured the country for six months, tub-thumping for her movies and fanning the sales of her dolls. And her dolls did sell. What happened to all the money, some of which Baby Peggy was supposed to receive, is not so clear. The star's father disagreed with Lesser about the numbers, and Baby Peggy moved on to vaudeville and eventually to adolescence. Her film career never again attained the heights of popularity it had reached during the 1920s. But she grew up as gracefully as possible and became a writer. The Baby Peggy dolls, however, will stay about five years old forever.

"It's an odd experience to hold a doll made in one's image a lifetime after its creation. However, for me, the feeling is not an emotional one. I have no regrets about not being Baby Peggy anymore, and I believe the doll filled a very real need for the children who owned them. Dolls never change—child stars do. Baby Peggy fans—and Shirley Temple fans as well—wanted to keep us little girls.

They wanted to pretend they were having tea with us or could take us for a stroll. But we grew up, taking all our childish cuteness with us and sadly disappointing them. As one child star's zealous fan once complained to me, 'I think it was positively wicked of Deanna Durbin to grow up!'"

Diana Serra Cary

The Patsy Family

PATSY WAS THE FIRST AMERICAN-MADE mass-produced doll to actually look like a child, with proportions that were fairly accurate. She was the first doll to have an extensive wardrobe and custom accessories. And she was the first doll to have a large extended family.

Patsy was about fourteen inches tall. Her hair was molded and painted a reddish brown. Her eyes were painted brown or, rarely, blue. She had chubby cheeks and a tiny mouth, as if she were trying to awaken a note from a reluctant horn. Although Patsy was known as "she," occasionally the same doll came dressed as a boy.

In 1928, the year Patsy began to come into her own, Effanbee produced a doll of Skippy, the hero of Percy Crosby's comic strip. Effanbee's Skippy, although advertised as the "Boy Friend of Patsy," was the same size as Patsy and, indeed, resembled in stance and attitude his girl friend. He was a close copy of

These two Patsy dolls were part of a great family that included almost a score of related dolls, ranging from Wee Patsy to Patsy Lou to Patsy Ruth.

the cartoon. He had molded blond hair with a curl on his fore-head. During World War II, the Skippy doll was outfitted in a U.S. Army uniform.

Patsy was so successful that within a couple of years a shelf of relatives—a family of spin-offs—emerged from the Effanbee factory. There was Patsykins, a few inches shorter, but still Patsy through and through. You could buy Patsykins as twins, one dressed as a boy, the other his sister. There was Patsy Babyette, born in 1930 and only nine inches tall. This doll, who also came as a boy or a girl, had curved arms and legs so she could hug just like a real baby.

Patsyette appeared in 1931. About nine inches tall, she was simply a smaller version of Patsy. She was "The Lovable Imp with tiltable head and movable limb," according to her heart-shaped Effanbee wrist tag. Some of the Patsyettes had mohair wigs anchored to the tops of their heads over their molded hair.

Patsy Joan was ten inches tall and looked a little older than Patsyette. Patricia was a few inches shorter than Patsy Joan and, like her, usually had a mohair wig. Mary Lee looked like the rest, except her mouth was open. Patsy Tinyette was the baby of the bunch. She was only six and a half inches long and came in a wicker trunk with a mattress, some extra gowns, and a nursing bottle. It can be confusing, but amusing, to keep track of all the Patsy dolls. There was also Patsy Ann and Patsy Lou, Patsy Ruth, and Patsy Mae, the doll Shirley Temple clutches in the movie *Captain January*. Many of the leading doll manufacturers of the day tried to compete with Patsy's success, and there were numerous copies.

In 1946 Effanbee reissued the doll that started all this fuss. "She's lovable, she's adorable, she's petite," read an advertisement. One of the nicest features about this doll was "her satin-smooth skin finish which gives a most lifelike effect." That was the new wonder material of the day—plastic. Her postwar price was three dollars and ninety-five cents.

Almost fifty years later, in 1995, Patsy Joan was brought out again by Effanbee. The price was higher, but the bobbed hair and the face were the same. And again she was a bestseller.

Mary Hoyer Dolls

A MARY HOYER DOLL was the "Best Dressed Doll in America," because the girl who owned her made her clothes (with, perhaps, her mother's help).

Mary Hoyer was a designer of knitted and crocheted clothes for children. She then came up with the idea of marketing matching outfits for the children's dolls. She created kits that contained the necessary materials along with instructions for making the clothes. The first dolls to wear Mary Hoyer outfits were made by the Ideal Novelty and Toy Company in 1925. The arrangement with Ideal lasted less than a year. Then Mary Hoyer designed her own doll, hired the well-known designer Bernard Lipfert to create a prototype, and arranged for the Fiberoid Doll Company to produce the dolls.

The first official Mary Hoyer doll was fourteen inches tall and made of composition. She had painted eyes. This unnamed doll was available until after World War II, when Hoyer had the doll made in plastic. A walking Hoyer doll was available for a short time. The first Hoyer doll with a name was Gigi, who was produced by the Frisch Doll Company in the early 1950s. Only about two thousand of them were produced.

In the late 1950s and during the next decade, the Mary Hoyer dolls increased in popularity. Except for Hoyer's own stores in Reading, Pennsylvania, and Atlantic City, New Jersey, her dolls were sold through the mail. By this time, each doll had a name. There was Vicky, manufactured by Ideal. She came in three sizes—ten and a half, twelve, and fourteen inches. She was made of vinyl and had a "perfectly formed body that turns, bends, bows from the waist." She was dressed in a brassiere, panties, high-heeled sandals, and earrings and cost only two dollars and fifty cents. In 1958 Margie made an appearance, and three years later there was Cathy. Later, after the hard-plastic Hoyer dolls were discontinued, Becky appeared. She was available in four hair colors and her hair could be washed, set, and combed in many styles. By all

Both of these hard-plastic Mary Hoyer dolls are fourteen inches tall and are dressed in their original costumes.

accounts, Becky was the most popular vinyl doll in the Hoyer line until the company ceased operations in 1968.

Although the dolls certainly were important to thousands of their "big sisters," the clothes that could be made were the major and distinguishing attraction of the Mary Hoyer dolls.

"Every little girl loves a doll. But wait 'til you see the expression on the child who cuddles closely THIS ADORABLE DOLL WEARING THE STUNNING CLOTHES KNIT OR CROCHETED WITH YOUR OWN HANDS. Your handiwork will add so much to the treasure!" read an advertisement in the 1948 *McCall's Needlework* magazine. The doll was priced at two dollars. An additional twenty-five cents was the cost of a copy of Mary Hoyer's Original Designs for Infants and Juveniles, which had thirty-two pages of "easy instructions for knitting and crocheting." And free with each doll was a copy of Mary's Dollies, a booklet with instructions for making six costumes.

There seemed no end to the outfits that could be made for a Mary Hoyer doll. Each doll had an outfit suited to her, or, perhaps, each outfit gave the doll her name and identity. There was a pattern for a princess dress for Goldilocks. A ski suit and matching cap for Juliana could be knitted: "The vest carries out the Norwegian motif and adds a dash of color," explained the preface to the knitting instructions. For Arlene there was a bathing ensemble, and for Olga a four-piece skating outfit.

One especially popular doll, Miss Victory, played a number of roles. She could be dressed as Zorina, "a charming (Russian) ally," as Sunny, the Queen of the Courts, or as Janie, a Modern Cinderella.

There were travel costumes, kits for a ballet costume, a Southern belle "masterpiece," playtime togs, even an elaborate Dolly Madison gown.

In 1995, production began once again and new Mary Hoyer dolls entered the market.

Madame Alexander Dolls

Meg is all cloth and fifteen inches tall. She was one of the dolls inspired by the novel "Little Women."

TO GENERATIONS OF WOMEN BEATRICE ALEXANDER needs no introduction. "It's a Madame Alexander—That's All You Need To Know" was the slogan printed on the boxes that held the prettiest and most beautifully dressed of dolls. From the early Alice in Wonderland dolls to the prized Little Women dolls to the recently re-released "classic" dolls of the 1950s, the Alexander Company produced many of the most beloved dolls of the century. If you played with dolls, it is likely at least one of them was a Madame Alexander doll.

Beatrice Alexander Behrman was born on March 9, 1895, the eldest of four daughters of a Russian immigrant who opened the first doll hospital in the United States. Beatrice was always artistic, and when World War I interrupted the import of bisque dolls from Germany she demonstrated her talent for seizing opportunity when she designed and made Red Cross nurse dolls, then, later, Alice in Wonderland dolls, which she sold in her father's shop.

In 1923, she founded the Alexander Doll Company and adopted the appellation Madame, giving her signature and her products a status she made sure they deserved. An early success was her dolls inspired by the novel *Little Women*. Other storybook dolls followed. In the middle of the Great Depression, Alexander scored the coup of the decade when she secured exclusive rights to manufacture a set of authorized Dionne Quintuplet dolls. Then, two years before the film version of *Gone With the Wind* was made, she designed and produced a Scarlett O'Hara doll because she thought the novel was wonderful. By the time the film was released to enormous critical acclaim, she had exclusive rights to manufacture the dolls.

Alexander's dolls of the 1930s were made of composition. She switched to plastic after World War II. The plastic dolls produced by the Alexander Doll Company during the 1950s are considered to be among the most beautifully designed and outfitted dolls in the industry.

Complementing Alexander's canny business sense and her energy was a renowned insistence on quality. The costumes she designed and produced for her dolls were their defining

Madame Alexander's cloth dolls, like Nell, right, and Meg, opposite page, were sold by mail order and in upscale candy shops.

element and are still considered the best in the business. This, combined with her instinct for getting good publicity, made her an almost legendary figure even outside the confines of the toy industry. She was one of a very few doll makers whose name was recognized and favored by the general public.

In 1953, Alexander was commissioned to make dolls commemorating the coronation of Queen Elizabeth of England. The thirty-six dolls were magnificently dressed, with careful attention paid to the smallest details. The dolls were shown on television before the ceremonies and were widely exhibited. Today, they are the keystone of the doll collection of the Brooklyn Children's Museum in New York. In 1965, on United Nations Day, Alexander was honored for her International Doll Collection—a group of eight-inch dolls authentically dressed in the costumes of every member country of the United Nations. The dolls produced by the Alexander Company are in the collections of the Smithsonian Institution in Washington, D.C., and in almost every doll museum, and museum with a doll collection, in the nation, as well as in museums abroad.

The Alexander dolls, however, are not yet relics. After the death of Beatrice Alexander, at the age of ninety, in 1990, the company floundered. Five years later it was bought by an investment team, Kaizen Breakthrough Partnership. At the factory in Harlem, New York, more than four hundred workers still produce dolls in the same hands-on way that they were made during Alexander's peak years.

The main line of dolls is prized by collectors (who make up about three-quarters of the company's customers), by doting grandmothers, and by mothers who are unable to part with their own Alexander dolls and buy similar dolls for their children.

The company still prints the old slogan on the dolls' boxes—"The Most Beautiful Dolls in the World Are by Madame Alexander." Millions of women of all ages agree.

Collector's Note

The prices for Madame Alexander dolls vary considerably with the age, desirability, and size of the doll. The early cloth dolls fetch from $200 to more than $1,000. Composition dolls range from $250 to well over $1,000. Most of the hard-plastic dolls, in excellent condition, average $500 to $600, but superb examples of especially rare or desirable dolls could be worth double that. The vinyl dolls range from $50 to $500.

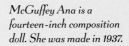

McGuffey Ana is a fourteen-inch composition doll. She was made in 1937.

Boudoir Dolls

LONG, THIN, CHIC, AND HAPPILY DECADENT, boudoir dolls were really decorations, not toys. Although, in passing, an advertisement would occasionally note that "some people buy her for the baby because she hasn't a hard spot in her," boudoir dolls, outfitted as if they were chief participants in a costume ball, added a flash of color and an air of worldliness to the parlor, the living room, or the bedroom.

Many if not most of these painted ladies—and it seems most were female figures, albeit highly stylized—were made entirely of cloth. Their faces were pressed and pinched and painted with theatrical features. Some of the dolls were imported from France and had composition limbs; others had composition heads and shoulders.

In the 1920s, the so-called Jazz Age, women were told by fashion and home magazines that "dolls with long dangling legs and arms in costumes reminiscent of the Louis periods in France are quite the vogue." One article included an illustration of a haughty doll dressed in a lavender silk and printed velvet flapper dress—not exactly a period costume—and satin shoes with heels so outrageously high as to be a joke. She cost eleven dollars and fifty cents.

The boudoir dolls were exotic and campy and designed for fun. Many of them were thirty or more inches tall. Their pliable, cotton-stuffed muslin bodies could be draped languidly against the pillows of a guest bed, in the corner of the sofa, or against the vanity mirror.

One popular boudoir doll was a Moor of regal yet evident jollity dressed in a yellow taffeta outfit with a matching turban. Another was supposed to be the actress Sarah Bernhardt lounging in white satin. You might have inherited one called Woops.

This beautifully gowned, demurely posed boudoir doll was designed to decorate a bedroom.

"He's the funniest thing you ever saw, Woops is. He looks like somebody's dreamt him," whooped an advertisement. "The stunts he can do with his long cretonne arms and his absurd boneless cretonne legs are enough to cheer up a party of mother-in-laws [sic]." The advertisement went on to explain that Woops could be a bridge prize or a Christmas tree ornament. He was thirty-four inches tall and cost two dollars and fifty cents. "No Matter What Else You Have for Xmas You Must Have a Woops," the advertisement concluded.

The cretonne of which Woops was made had an oriental floral design or a solid color combination. The doll had slanted eyes, a simple cartoon nose, and a smile. Woops wore a bandanna and what looked like a loincloth. If Woops's clothes (or lack of them) were too casual for the parlor or sitting room, a variety of outfits were available, from a "tight bodice, bouffant skirt, long pantalettes, and wide-brimmed bonnet to match" to the latest thing in pajamas.

Boudoir dolls were supposed to be dressed to match the color schemes of the rooms they decorated. Many of the magazines that carried advertisements for the dolls also had advertisements for additional costumes. For those who didn't want to pay for a decorative doll and were handy with fabric and needle and thread, there were boudoir-doll kits available in stores and by mail from various women's magazines. As late as 1934, it was possible to send away for an undressed doll, as well as fabric and directions to make a dress.

Boudoir dolls were so fashionable that they frequently appeared in advertisements for such products as corsets, the latest ethnic blouses, or—the height of the good life—French chocolates, Bonbons, and Favors by Louis Sherry.

Bejeweled, heavily made up, and dressed in red lace, this doll was obviously intended to look sophisticated and a bit campy.

Bonnie Babe

BONNIE BABE WAS ONE OF HUNDREDS of dolls designed by Georgene Averill for Averill Manufacturing Company in the first half of the twentieth century. Averill was famous for her Bonnie Babe and Mama dolls, and for her unusual method of promoting them.

In 1913 Georgene Averill created her first line of dolls. She and her husband, Paul, bought dolls that had composition heads and cloth bodies and dressed them as character dolls in felt costumes. In 1918, Averill obtained U.S. patents for four doll costumes: a Dutch girl, a cowboy, an Indian papoose, and an Indian girl.

Rather than make her own dolls, Averill continued to buy high-quality dolls from other doll makers and to dress them in her patented costumes. One advantage of this was that she could choose different faces for the various characters, so that all the dolls didn't look the same.

Averill's next project was a line of American babies and little girls dressed in popular styles. Known as the Lyf-Lyk line, it included one hundred and fifty dolls dressed in long and short dresses made from a variety of fabrics.

One of Averill's most important breakthroughs came in 1918, when she patented her walking Mama doll. Although this was one of the first American Mama dolls, its popularity stemmed from the improved design. Averill's Mama doll had arms and legs that moved without mechanical joints. The secret was in the body design and the loose hip and shoulder stitching, which allowed the limbs to move. Of course, the doll's owner had to help by holding the doll and swinging her body just so, but nevertheless, in the 1920s Averill's walking doll was considered innovative. Today, designers still use the same basic design for cloth-body dolls.

One of Georgene Averill's earliest Bonnie Babes, this twelve-and-a half-inch doll has a German bisque head, a cloth body, and celluloid hands.

Bonnie Babe, a baby doll, was introduced by Georgene Averill around 1920. The doll had a bisque, celluloid, or composition head; flange neck; molded and painted features; brown hair; brown glass eyes that opened and closed; and an open mouth with two lower teeth. The body was cloth. The arms and legs were composition or celluloid. Bonnie Babe also had a voice box. She came in a variety of sizes; the largest is generally the most valuable today.

The all-bisque Bonnie Babe dates from 1926 and was made entirely from molded bisque, jointed at the head, arms, and legs. The design was similar to the previous Bonnie Babe, except that the bisque feet were encased in molded slippers painted pink or blue. The all-bisque version was unmarked except for a paper label on her stomach, and came in two sizes: five and seven inches.

Walking Mama, Bonnie Babe, and many other dolls were created under Averill's pseudonym—Madame Hendren—and sold at her Fifth Avenue store in New York City. Like the Cabbage Patch Kids many decades later, Averill's baby dolls were displayed in carefully designed settings. She originated this promotional method with her character dolls, which were demonstrated at department stores by young women dressed in costumes identical to those worn by the dolls. As early as 1916, the dolls took center stage in store windows, frolicking in artfully created scenes.

At Averill's store, salesclerks dressed as nurses talked to and played with the dolls as if they were really children. Of course, it helped that the dolls could respond with their childlike "Mama." In 1923, *Playthings* magazine reported that 80 percent of buyers' requests for dolls were for Averill's Mama dolls.

Georgene Averill designed many other dolls, including Dolly Reckord, which had a record-playing mechanism; Body Twist Dimmie and Jimmie, which had jointed waists; and characters like Snookums, Little Lulu, Nancy, Sluggo, and Tubby Tom. But Georgene Averill was best known for Bonnie Babe, walking Mama dolls, and her clever store promotions.

Only five inches tall, this Bonnie Babe is made entirely of bisque.

43

1930–1939

THE YEARS OF THE 1930S ARE ASSOCIATED with the Great Depression. Beginning in 1929 and lasting through most of the next decade, the economic status of most Americans diminished. After years and years of tumultuous change, the prosperous times were suddenly over and there was widespread unemployment.

By the mid-1930s, news reports from the rest of the world were sobering. Hitler and Mussolini were coming to power in Europe and militarists were in control in Japan. The United States had a stated policy of isolationism, and many people urged pacifism. As a result of President Franklin Delano Roosevelt's New Deal, social welfare programs were initiated to give jobs to the unemployed. One of the Works Projects Administration (WPA) projects was designed for people who were skilled in the arts. WPA dolls were made under grants to several states. (Towns, states, colleges, and museums could write a project and apply for a grant.) These dolls are collectibles now because they were handmade.

During this time of economic hardship, millions of people

thronged to movie theaters as an escape from reality. Capitalizing on Hollywood's popularity, the American toy industry produced some of its most successful dolls. The Ideal Novelty and Toy Company realized that the charisma of the dimpled, curly-headed young Shirley Temple made her a perfect subject for a doll. They brought out the composition Shirley Temple doll in 1934, and she became extremely popular. Naturally, other doll manufacturers, seeing the success of that doll, made their own Shirley look-alikes. The Shirley Temple doll was such a resounding success that manufacturers began to make dolls of other child stars, including Jane Withers, Anne Shirley, Deanna Durbin, and Judy Garland.

The movies also inspired doll companies to make dolls of fictional characters. *Gone With the Wind*, Disney's *Snow White and the Seven Dwarfs*, and *The Wizard of Oz* all caught the public's fancy. Scarlett O'Hara has been the subject of many dolls, but the first ones were by the Alexander Doll Company. And Madame Beatrice Alexander was the first doll maker to license a name to use for a doll.

The Gerber Baby Doll

THE GERBER BABY HAS A FACE that has launched untold millions of containers of food specially prepared for babies. Commercial baby food was a new concept in 1930 when Dorothy Gerber, the wife of the president of a canning company in Fremont, Michigan, had the idea of relieving mothers of the work of cooking and straining food for their infants. Then, in response to an advertising campaign to find just the right baby to publicize the new line, Dorothy Hope, an artist, submitted a charcoal drawing of Ann Turner, the baby daughter of a neighbor. In 1931, little Ann's face became the officially registered trademark of Gerber baby food—the Gerber Baby.

The first Gerber Baby dolls appeared in 1936. They were made of sateen (pink for girls, blue for boys) and had silk-screened faces. Each doll held a plush "can" of baby food and a toy duck or dog. The babies, about eight inches tall, were stuffed with cotton. To get a doll, all that was necessary was to return a coupon from a Gerber baby food advertisement, along with a dime and labels from three Gerber baby food containers. The girl dolls were shipped in pink boxes, the boys in blue. Accompanying each doll was an advertising insert. (At that time, in addition to cereal, there were only eight varieties of strained baby food: vegetable soup, carrots, spinach, beets, green beans, prunes, peas, and tomatoes.) That first Gerber Baby offer ran for three years, during which more than twenty-six thousand dolls were shipped.

The next Gerber premium doll was made in 1955 by the Sun Rubber Company. It was twelve inches tall, had "drink and wet" capability, a crying mechanism, jointed arms and

The head and hands of this twelve-inch Gerber Baby are made of hard vinyl. The body is cuddly cloth. The baby's clothes, the pillow, and the basket are all original.

legs, and a soft vinyl head that could turn. The baby, dressed in a diaper and a bib, came with a glass bottle with a rubber nipple, miniature Gerber cereal boxes, a cereal dish, and a spoon. All this for two dollars and twelve Gerber baby food labels.

Sun Rubber also produced fourteen- and eighteen-inch Gerber Babies, which, for the three years of the premium campaign, were sold through Sears, Roebuck catalogs and in toy shops and department stores.

There was another premium Gerber Baby from 1966 to 1968. It was almost identical to the 1955 baby and the cost was the same.

In 1971 and 1972 two more Gerber Baby premium dolls were made. Amsco Industries produced a ten-inch white baby the first year of the campaign and a ten-inch African-American baby the second year. Both dolls were vinyl, fully jointed, and had painted eyes. These dolls didn't come with bottles, but they were dressed in cotton sleepers. They cost two dollars and fifty cents and four labels from any Gerber Toddler Meal, Strained or Junior High Meat Dinner, or two box tops from Gerber fruit cereals.

In 1979, Gerber celebrated its fiftieth anniversary and there was a new Gerber Baby doll, the first that was not a company premium. This baby, the work of sculptor Neil Estern, was seventeen inches tall, soft-bodied, and had sandy-colored molded hair. Estern was also responsible for the porcelain head of the soft-bodied, beautifully dressed Gerber Baby Limited Edition Collector's Doll that was made in 1983.

In 1996 the Gerber Baby doll was back in the stores again. To be in step with the times, four variations were introduced— Feel Better Baby, Loving Tears Baby, Potty Time Baby, and Tub Time Baby. Each twenty-inch doll comes with accessories appropriate to its name. And they all have little Ann Turner's adorable face.

In 1972, the Gerber baby doll was African American. This doll looks more like a toddler than an infant. She has eyes that roll from side to side and are known as "flirty eyes."

Shirley Temple

Collector's Note

Some doll collectors specialize in Shirley Temple dolls, so there is always a demand for these dolls even though there are still a fair number on the market. Ideal's composition dolls from the 1930s tend to be priced between $800 and $1,000, depending on size and condition. The plastic and vinyl dolls from the 1950s average $200 to $300, unless they are very large. The 1970s vinyl dolls might be worth $100 or more. A variety of Shirleys were made through the years and many Shirley "look-alikes" must be evaluated on an individual basis.

"The Official Doll of the Texas Centennial," made of composition, came out in 1936. Later she was simply called the "Shirley Temple Texas Ranger Doll."

SHIRLEY TEMPLE, the child star who illuminated the silver screen, was a bright spot in the bleak grayness of the Great Depression. The doll she inspired brightened the lives of hundreds and thousands of children.

Shirley Temple, the doll, was introduced to little girls throughout the country in 1934, the year Shirley Temple, the six-year-old actress, became a national film phenomenon.

The Ideal Novelty and Toy Company had scored one of the great merchandising coups of all time. After months of negotiations with Temple's parents, the company secured an exclusive contract to produce a doll of the movie star. Ideal had the body (they had perfected a lifelike torso the year before for a doll called Ginger) but, reportedly, the designer Bernard Lipfert had to make twenty molds before the head was finally approved by everyone involved.

The first costume for the Shirley doll portrayed the actress as she looked performing "Baby Take a Bow" in *Stand Up and Cheer*, her movie of that year. This inaugural doll had a slightly chubbier face than the real Shirley. The faces of the later dolls were slimmed down. At first the doll was made in four sizes, with prices ranging from three to seven dollars.

The Shirley Temple doll was perfect for a marketing campaign of

Hollywood proportions. In 1936, according to the industry trade journal *Playthings,* Ideal pitched "one of the largest national promotions ever undertaken by any doll or toy manufacturer." A contest was announced in the comic strip sections of fourteen million Sunday newspapers, along with an advertisement for the doll, of course. The top ten prizes were real Scottish terrier puppies like Shirley Temple's pet Corky. Other prizes included such doll accessories as clothes and carriages.

Ideal's Shirley Temple was not only the most popular celebrity doll ever made, she was also the most copied. Nearly everybody tried to get in on the act. Even the renowned doll maker Madame Alexander, after publicly opposing the exploitation of Shirley Temple's fame as an actress, produced a Little Colonel doll in 1935. Alexander maintained that her doll was inspired by the children's book on which the character was based. It just so happened that the appearance of the doll coincided with the release of Shirley Temple's movie *The Little Colonel,* and the doll looked very much like Ideal's Shirley.

By 1939, as the Depression drew to a close and the dark clouds of World War II gathered, Shirley Temple's reign as a box-office queen was over. That year, Ideal ceased production of the doll. Never a company to turn its back on success, however, Ideal used some of the Shirley molds for other dolls, including Snow White.

The Shirley Temple doll made a comeback in the 1950s in vinyl and plastic. Then, in the 1970s, she took another bow. Like her movies, Shirley Temple doesn't age.

This vinyl Shirley Temple doll was made in the 1950s by the Ideal Toy Corporation.

49

Other Celebrity Dolls

Deanna Durbin

IN HOLLYWOOD THE EARLY TEENS HAVE ALWAYS been considered the age when a child star must retire, at least temporarily. Deanna Durbin was the great exception. She became a star at the age of fourteen when her first picture for Universal, *Three Smart Girls*, grossed two million dollars and saved the studio from bankruptcy. The following year her beautiful voice and natural charm made *100 Men and a Girl* an equally big success. She quickly became the highest paid film actress in the country, earning a then astronomical three hundred thousand dollars a year.

Deanna Durbin's face, as lovely as her voice, appeared on magazine covers and sheet music. There were Deanna Durbin coloring books and paper dolls. And, of course, there was a Deanna Durbin doll. It was manufactured by Ideal Novelty and Toy Company in 1938, when Deanna was seventeen years old. The company claimed that this was the first teenage doll in toy history. There were versions from fourteen to twenty-five inches tall. The doll was all composition, fully jointed, and had dark brown human hair and green sleep eyes with long lashes. Her mouth was slightly open, revealing tiny white teeth. She was dressed in a cotton dress with a floral pattern. On the dress was a pin with a picture of the real Deanna Durbin and the word "doll" underneath the photo. Other outfits were available, many of them drawn from Deanna's film roles. They were considered spectacular when they first came out and they are prized today by collectors. There were long fancy party dresses, two-piece suits with matching berets, and outfits with bolero jackets. As each new movie was released, so were new outfits. And with each doll, you got a glossy photograph of Deanna for your Hollywood scrapbook.

Deanna Durbin successfully made the transition to adult film actress and had dramatic roles in a number of movies, including *Christmas Holiday*, in which she played Gene Kelly's accessory in crime. Then, at the age of twenty-seven, she retired.

This all-composition Deanna Durbin has her original metal button with her picture and the inscription: "Deanna Durbin She's a Doll!"

Sonja Henie

SONJA HENIE WAS DIMINUTIVE, BEAUTIFUL, AND BLOND, with a smile that could melt an iceberg. Born in Oslo, Norway, in 1912, she learned to dance and ski by the time she was five years old. She took to ice skates the next year and four years later, when she was ten years old, she won her country's national ice-skating championship. And that was only the beginning.

By the time she was twenty-four, Sonja Henie had won the world ice-skating championships ten years in a row and had garnered three consecutive Olympic gold medals. After the 1936 Olympics she turned professional and toured the United States with an ice show, setting and breaking attendance records wherever she performed.

She skated into the movies in 1936 with *One in a Million*, and in this and her eleven subsequent feature films, she was always the star and her name got billing above the title. After she became a movie star, Sonja Henie's ice shows were more popular than ever. She began endorsing products, including parkas, mittens, skates, and dolls.

The Alexander Doll Company made Sonja Henie dolls for about four years, beginning in 1939. Actually, Alexander assembled, dressed, and marketed the dolls. The doll itself was designed for the company by Bernard Lipfert. An anonymous manufacturer poured the molds and made the parts, then shipped them on to Alexander.

None of that would have interested the girls who wanted to find Sonja Henie under their Christmas trees. The dolls were produced in a number of sizes, from thirteen and a half to twenty-one inches tall. They were made of composition and fully jointed. They had brown sleep eyes, an open mouth with four to six teeth, depending on the size of the doll, and blond wigs, some of human hair, some of mohair. All the dolls had dimples, just like the real Sonja Henie.

The Sears Christmas Catalog of 1939 showed a Sonja Henie doll gliding on ice, a spotlight shining down on her. According to the catalog, the dolls were sold by mail only by Sears and wore a "flared velveteen skirt - cap - undies - panties - white imitation leather shoe skates. Blonde human hair wig. Glass-like sleeping eyes." Other dolls shown in the advertisement, evidently watching

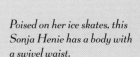

Poised on her ice skates, this Sonja Henie has a body with a swivel waist.

*Made by Effanbee in the late
1930s, this fifteen-inch Anne
Shirley is composition, has a
wig of human hair, and is
wearing her original dress.*

Sonja, were Judy Garland (as Dorothy in *The Wizard of Oz*), Cinderella, and Deanna Durbin.

In the December 9, 1940, issue of *Life,* a two-page spread showed the Sonja doll in fifteen costumes including a girdle, a four-piece sports outfit, a ski suit trimmed with marabou, a crepe nightgown and negligee, a bridal gown, and, most important, a hand-knit skating outfit.

After World War II, as Sonja Henie's career began to fade, Alexander came out with skating dolls, like Babs, the Ice-Skating Girl, that looked like Sonja Henie dolls but didn't have her name. The Sonja Henie doll, plastic with a vinyl head, did make a comeback in 1951. By this time, Sonja Henie's movie career was over. She died of leukemia in 1969. Like the title of her first film, and like your very own Sonja Henie, she was one in a million.

Anne Shirley

ANNE SHIRLEY WAS A DOLL who could play enough roles to satisfy the most ambitious actress. She was a young movie star. She was also a model for historic fashions, an ice-skater, an innocent youngster, and a mature, worldly woman.

Appropriately, the doll was originally created as Anne of Green Gables, one of Anne Shirley's most famous roles. Capitalizing on the 1934 film *Anne of Green Gables*, Effanbee put long red hair on some of its Patsy Joan dolls and dressed them in costumes from the movie. That first Anne Shirley was about fifteen inches tall and had brown or green eyes that opened and closed. She had red human hair, or mohair, styled in pigtails. She wore a country print dress and matching straw hat. The next year, in an attempt to compete with Ideal's popular Shirley Temple doll, Effanbee came out with an Anne Shirley doll that looked more like the actress who starred in *Anne of Green Gables*.

The young actress's real name was

Dawn Evelyeen Paris. She was a photographer's model at eighteen months old and started her career in the movies before she was four. She was known as Dawn O'Day and appeared in about fifty silent shorts and early talkies. In 1934, she was tapped by the director George Nicholas Jr. to play the lead in *Anne of Green Gables.* Reportedly, by contract, she had to take the name Anne Shirley to play the lead character, Anne Shirley.

Over the years the Anne Shirley doll came in different sizes, with a variety of wigs, and different kinds of eyes. One of the doll's most memorable roles was the star of a pageant of historical figures. They included 1658—The Carolina Settlement; 1720—the Pioneering American Spirit, and 1682—the Quaker Colony. The final entry in the series was 1939—Today. This doll was blond, with a pageboy hairstyle and brown eyes. She wore a Coco Chanel gown—purple skirt, white bodice with lots of ruffles, and green sash. Beginning in the late 1930s, the Anne Shirley doll was also sold under another name— Little Lady.

During the 1940s, Anne Shirley's fame as child star faded. She managed however, to proceed gracefully into adult roles, retiring from show business at the age of twenty-five, immediately after what many critics claim was her best performance, starring opposite Dick Powell in the 1945 movie *Murder, My Sweet.*

Jane Withers

JANE WITHERS BEGAN PERFORMING in 1930 when she was four years old. She got her start in films when she was six. After *Bright Eyes,* in which she appeared with Shirley Temple, Withers's roles began to change from tomboy to leading lady. In 1938 she was ranked number eight at the box office.

Madame Alexander's Jane Withers doll captured the impish expression of the child star.

In 1937 Madame Alexander began to make the Jane Withers doll. Although Withers was eleven years old at the time, the doll looked younger, in part because she wore the then popular short "baby doll" dresses. Nevertheless, the doll

Collector's Note

A Judy Garland doll
can bring over $1,000
if her composition is
in perfect condition
and she has her
original clothes.

was a good likeness of Withers. An advertisement in the 1937 Sears Christmas Book described the doll as "the lovable imp of the movies created into a laughing, adorable human-looking doll. And not one bit of her bubbling enthusiasm, warming smile, saucy spirit has been lost in the process."

The all-composition, fully jointed doll came in four sizes: thirteen and a half, fifteen, seventeen, and twenty inches. She had a reddish-brown mohair wig with curls and bangs, brown eyes, and lashes. Variations had dark red hair, green eyes, sleep eyes, or different mouths.

The Jane Withers doll sold through the Sears, Roebuck catalog wore a "lace trimmed dress, cute hat with saucy, turned brim. Lace undies, rayon socks, snap buckle shoes. . . ." Most of the dolls also had a gold-tone metal pin that spelled "Jane Withers" in script.

After her doll days, Withers's roles gradually decreased, and she retired at the age of twenty-one to raise a family. She played bit parts in *Giant* in 1956 and in *Captain Newman, M.D.* in 1964. She then had a twelve-year stint as "Josephine," the plumber who pitched Comet cleanser in television commercials.

Jane Withers is still active in Hollywood today, albeit not on the screen. She has dedicated many years to helping the Hollywood Museum become a reality by collecting memorabilia from old movie sets. She has also shared her fabulous doll collection with television audiences.

Judy Garland

IN 1939, *THE WIZARD OF OZ* WAS RELEASED with enormous fanfare and great critical acclaim. Almost simultaneously a portrait doll of Judy Garland, the eighteen-year-old actress who played the heroine, Dorothy, appeared in stores across the country. Designed by Bernard Lipfert, the famous doll artist, this likeness of Judy Garland was dressed as Dorothy in the film. She wore a blue-and-white-checked pinafore over a white organdy blouse. Some dolls appeared in the stores dressed in a red dress and white apron, the outfit described by L. Frank Baum in the book upon which the film was based.

Many other Judy Garland dolls appeared through the years. Ideal produced a Judy Garland teen doll dressed in the white gown from Judy's 1940 musical *Strike Up the Band.* Her next movie, *Babes on Broadway,* inspired yet another doll. But these dolls had nowhere near the success of those that depicted Garland as Dorothy.

In 1958, a hard-plastic Judy Garland doll, dressed as Dorothy, was released by Ideal to coincide with the first television screening of *The Wizard of Oz.* This doll was not nearly as popular as the original one.

This eighteen-inch composition Judy Garland doll,
circa 1939, is costumed as Dorothy of "The Wizard of Oz."
Made by Ideal, she is treasured by collectors of dolls,
movie memorabilia, and popular culture.

Dionne Quintuplets

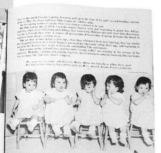

IN A HAMLET IN ONTARIO, CANADA, on May 28, 1934, at four o'clock in the morning, Elzire Dionne gave birth to five girls. The babies were about two months premature and each one weighed about two pounds. The infants were wrapped in blankets and placed in a borrowed wicker basket.

Doctor Allan Roy Dafoe, the physician who attended three of the births (two local midwives had delivered the first two babies earlier), didn't think the babies would live, so he took it upon himself to baptize them on the spot. He sent for a priest to administer last rites to the mother, who didn't look as if she would survive either.

The mother and the five baby girls did survive. At that time, when there were no fertility drugs, the probability of a quintuplet birth was about one in fifty-seven million. And when there was such a birth it was rare for the mother and all the infants to live. These babies were the first quintuplets to survive for more than fifty minutes. It was considered a miracle.

Marie. Yvonne. Annette. Emilie. Cecile. There was a time almost everybody knew those names. Everything the babies did was recorded by newspapers around the world. Each birthday was an event. If one child cut a tooth, had a cold, did anything in any way cute, the story made the papers, was mentioned on the radio and shown in newsreels. Photographs of the five were ubiquitous. Romanticized illustrations of the infants appeared on calendars (from Canada, The Land of the Quintuplets) and magazine covers. Their home and the nursery, built by the Canadian government, was called Quintland, and drew hundreds and thousands of the curious, who gazed at the sisters through one-way observation glass.

The quintuplets ignited a merchandising industry. There were endorsements galore and their pictures appeared on an array of products. Dionne Quintuplet dolls were a natural and almost immediate avenue of exploitation. It has been said that the sisters were the best real subjects for dolls ever. After all, the customer would surely buy all five.

From 1935 to 1939 the Alexander Doll Company produced the only authentic Dionne Quintuplet dolls. Beatrice Alexander secured a secret agreement with the numerous guardians of the sisters, nailing down exclusive rights to dolls advertised with the Dionne name. The first Dionne dolls appeared in time for Christmas 1935. Alexander also made a fourteen-and-a-half-inch "Doctor Doll for the Quints" and a "Nurse Doll for the Quints."

Smaller, less expensive dolls were sold as sets. The larger dolls, ranging in size from twelve to twenty-three inches, were sold separately. The little babies were made of composition. The larger dolls had composition limbs and cloth bodies. The sisters as toddlers were all composition. They wore name tags and each quintuplet doll had her own color for her outfits: Marie wore blue, Yvonne wore pink, Annette wore yellow, Emilie wore lavender, and Cecile wore green.

A phenomenon like the quintuplets was sure to attract copies and imitations. Effanbee's Baby Tinyettes were marketed in sets of five. The Arranbee Doll Company also produced its quintuplets. The dolls were not marked or advertised as Dionne Quintuplets, but there was no doubt whom they represented.

As the five sisters grew up, the searing spotlight dimmed. As adolescents, and as adults, they were not as "cute" and not as malleable. Society lost interest. A world war was more important. The newspaper clippings, the calendars, the gewgaws, and the dolls were relegated to attics and rummage sales. Only collectors continued to care.

Collector's Note

A Dionne doll with the cloth body is currently worth about $700. With the all-composition body, a quintuplet can bring from $300 to $500 depending on the size of the doll. A set of the Dionne Quintuplets, wearing original clothing and, of course, in very good condition, is worth at least $1,500. The Dr. Dafoe doll is now worth about $800.

Madame Alexander's Quintuplets were composition, five and a half inches tall, and came in a personalized bed.

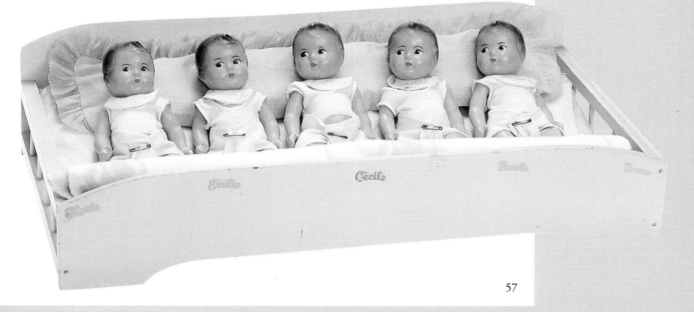

Snow White and the Seven Dwarfs

SNOW WHITE AND THE SEVEN DWARFS have been around for a long time. The best-known retelling was written by the Brothers Grimm. Through the years countless versions of this fairy tale have been published, but Walt Disney made the story his own in 1937. Shortly after the premier of the landmark movie, several toy and doll companies, including Ideal—which had a charming doll—Knickerbocker, and the Alexander Doll Company, transformed the characters into dolls.

Madame Alexander started making Snow White dolls in 1938 and the company is still at it. One of Alexander's most distinctive versions was the hard-plastic Snow White of the 1950s. Although this doll was merely another Alexander doll in costume, she did live up to Snow White's reputation of being the fairest in the land. R. G. Kruger made a set of cloth dolls. Gund, too, was a major manufacturer of Disney dolls. If you visited the Disney parks in the late 1970s, you might have carried away Snow White and the Dwarfs made by Effanbee.

To mark the movie's fiftieth anniversary, Disney re-released it with great fanfare. Doll manufacturers followed close behind the movie with new versions.

The seven little miners who shared the spotlight with Snow White were manufactured at her side. They could be bought as a set or singly. Ideal, Alexander, Gund, and R. G. Krueger were among the many toy and doll makers who produced versions of the characters—all of them drawing on the Disney version of the story.

Knickerbocker's Snow White is made of composition with molded hair.

In 1938 Ideal produced a notable set of composition and cloth Dwarfs that captured some of the fun of the characters and some of the style of Fred Moore, the animator. Unfortunately, the Snow White of that year doesn't measure up. She is a Shirley Temple doll dressed as Snow White, and she doesn't look like the princess of the movie.

Knickerbocker Toy Company of New York also produced a memorable set of characters. These dolls have painted features and hair, swivel heads, and jointed limbs. Snow White looks younger than her animated version (and truer to the Grimms' story in which the girl is only seven years old when she escapes into the forest). She wears a white taffeta dress with navy-blue velvet bodice, blue velvet cape with red silk, white pantaloons, white socks, and shoes. This Snow White is twelve inches tall; the Dwarfs are nine inches short and are dressed in velvet costumes. Each Dwarf (as was generally the case, regardless of the manufacturer) wore his name on his hat.

In 1976, Effanbee made a fine vinyl Snow White and cloth Dwarfs (with stocking faces) as part of the company's Storybook Doll Collection.

Snow White and the Seven Dwarfs are still being produced by a variety of manufacturers. The story, after all, is timeless, and the dolls will undoubtedly continue to enchant many new generations.

Chad Valley Company, Ltd., of England made this Snow White and the Seven Dwarfs in the late 1940s. Snow White is seventeen inches tall and the Dwarfs are nine and a half inches tall. All the dolls have painted features on pressed felt mask faces.

Nancy Ann Storybook Dolls

THE NANCY ANN STORYBOOK DOLLS were "wee dolls for wee collectors." Today they are wee dolls for grown-up collectors. They were made from 1936 until the mid-1960s, after which, for about twenty years, dolls bearing the Storybook name surfaced now and then.

Created by Nancy Ann Abbot and her business partner, Leslie Rowland, the Storybook Dolls are only three and a half to six and a half inches tall. The early ones, made from 1936 until 1948, were bisque. For the next two years the dolls were plastic. Some of the dolls produced in the latter half of the 1940s have bisque bodies and plastic arms. Then parts of the dolls, and later the complete dolls, were made of vinyl.

Like the bisque dolls, the plastic dolls had handpainted facial features (except when they had sleep eyes). Most of the plastic dolls also had movable arms, legs, and heads. The dolls that were only three and a half to four and a half inches tall had heads that were a molded part of the trunk.

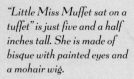

"Little Miss Muffet sat on a tuffet" is just five and a half inches tall. She is made of bisque with painted eyes and a mohair wig.

The Style Dolls by Abbot, widely held in high regard by fashion doll collectors, appeared in 1950. Priced from sixteen dollars to thirty-five dollars (Her Royal Majesty's Wedding), the Style Dolls were children dressed in grown-up fashions. The clothes are considered superb examples of miniature dressmaking. But the cost of producing such quality was too high, and the Style Dolls lasted only a few years. One of the most memorable was Lemon Frost, an eighteen-inch doll dressed in a long, light-yellow nylon dress and straw hat.

The Storybook Dolls came in more than a score of series. Little girls had to collect them all, or at least one from every

series, for example the Bridal series and the American Girls series, which included Quaker Maid, Colonial Dame, Southern Belle, and Western Miss. You might have had Debut, one of the Commencement series. She was blond with dark eyes and wore a long white dress trimmed with lots of lace, a white satin petticoat, long pantaloons, and black slippers. Perhaps you had Winter, from the Seasons series. She wore a long dark green taffeta dress. A red ribbon encircled her tiny waist. Under all that flounce, she wore long pantaloons and black painted slippers. On top of her abundant auburn hair sat a tiny black felt hat festooned with a red feather. Other series included Mother Goose, Fairy Tales, Dolls of the Day, Dolls of the Month (July, for example, was a blonde with black eyes who wore a long red and white dress and a red felt hat almost as big as she was), Operettas, Gardens, Jewels, and All-Time Hit Parades, starring "Stardust" and "Over the Rainbow."

If you were especially good—or, perhaps, especially naughty—you might have received a doll from the Religious series. One of these dolls was dressed as a nun. She wore a long habit with a black wimple. At her waist was a black cord from which a golden cross was suspended.

The Nancy Ann Storybook Doll Company was sold in 1966. Today, Storybook Dolls can be found at collectible shows and at doll shows in beautiful condition, their arms still open as if awaiting a hug, the frills on their dresses still starched and ruffly.

The Religious series included this six-inch Nun, with jointed limbs and sleep eyes, and "First Communion," made of hard plastic with painted white gloves and slippers.

"A girl for August when it's warm" is from the Dolls of the Month series. Just over six inches tall, this hard-plastic doll is dressed up for a summer party.

Charlie McCarthy

Thousands of youngsters who owned Charlie McCarthy dolls discovered that it isn't easy to be a ventriloquist.

CHARLIE MCCARTHY WAS A BRAT, A WISE GUY, and a smart aleck. Or, in the words of his great radio adversary, W. C. Fields, he was "a little squirrel's warehouse," "a termite's flophouse," and a "dead limb on the tree of knowledge."

Fields—or anyone else, for that matter—rarely had the last word with Charlie. "Why, you barfly," Charlie shot back at Fields, "I'll stick a wick in your mouth and use you for an alcohol lamp."

The first ventriloquist's dummy, basically a wooden doll with a movable mouth, was made in 1750 by a Baron Mengen of Austria. Since then, innumerable ventriloquists have entertained and amazed the public by creating the illusion that the dummy was speaking.

Charlie McCarthy, the world's most famous and most beloved ventriloquist's dummy, was created by Edgar Bergen in 1922 when he was a senior at Chicago's Lakeview High School. Every day, in front of the school, Bergen noticed a young Irish ruffian named Charlie selling newspapers. Bergen made a sketch of the boy and gave it and some construction specifications to a carpenter named Theodore Mack, who carved the dummy out of pine and charged Bergen about twenty-seven dollars. Bergen named the dummy Charlie McCarthy after the newsboy and the carpenter.

Edgar Bergen was a particularly talented ventriloquist and worked his way through college by performing across the United States and abroad, eventually rising to the top on the vaudeville circuit. When vaudeville died, Bergen and his dummy began performing in nightclubs. Charlie was outfitted in a tuxedo or tails. He had a monocle, a top hat, and an affected British accent. They were a smash hit.

By this time, the first Charlie had been replaced by the "real" Charlie, who was carved in Chicago by Frank Marshall and Alex Camero. The dummy's head and body frame were basswood. The limbs were stuffed with wood wool. Charlie's mouth, rolling eyes, and lids that could wink were operated by cords, a bulb, and a lever. Charlie's wardrobe was estimated to be worth a thousand dollars. (He wore a size 4 suit, size 2AAA shoes, and a $33^{3}/_{8}$ hat.)

Bergen was probably one of the most abused straight men of all time. Charlie had all the punch lines. He teased Bergen about his baldness, his dull wit, his parsimony, even the movement of his lips when he was giving voice to Charlie. Bergen's role was that of a gentle father figure, trying to teach his wooden charge how to behave. Fortunately for the delighted public, Charlie never learned.

A successful stint at the Rainbow Room in Manhattan led to a guest appearance on Rudy Vallee's radio show. A ventriloquist's act on radio certainly seemed implausible, but Bergen and Charlie were no ordinary performers. That first spot led to a thirteen-week run on Vallee's show, and then to their own show, the *Chase and Sanborn Hour* on NBC. Within a few years the show was rated one of the top three on the air and, frequently, number one in the country. The time was ripe for a Charlie McCarthy doll. In 1937 Effanbee announced that it had obtained permission to produce "an exact reproduction of the original Charlie McCarthy made famous by Edgar Bergen."

Effanbee's Charlie had a composition head, hands, and feet. His hinged mouth was operated by a pull string at the back of his head. He was available in three sizes: fifteen, seventeen, and twenty inches. Charlie was nattily attired in evening dress and top hat. In his left eye was that famous monocle. The doll, a striking figure, was designed by Virginia Austin, a puppet maker.

That same year, Ideal Novelty and Toy Company entered the picture with a nicely rendered Charlie McCarthy hand puppet with a composition head, a molded top hat, and painted features.

By 1939, a variety of outfits were available for Charlie, including a blue coat, white pants and cap; an overcoat, beret, and matching suit; and a complete riding habit, including the hat.

Charlie became a one-dummy industry. In his heyday there were Charlie McCarthy games, paper dolls, coloring books, puzzles, a tin windup toy, Charlie McCarthy birthday and Christmas cards, Charlie McCarthy banks, drinking glasses, comic books, small rubber dolls, and thousands of knockoff plaster statues and composition figures, usually cheap souvenirs or prizes at fairs and carnivals. And, as with many other successful dolls—and performers—there were numerous Charlie McCarthy copycats.

One of Bergen and Charlie's last appearances was in 1978 in a cameo in *The Muppet Movie*. Before the movie was released, Bergen officially announced his retirement and donated Charlie to the Smithsonian Institution in Washington, D.C. A few weeks later, Bergen died. *The Muppet Movie* is dedicated to Edgar Bergen.

Collector's Note

The condition of Charlie McCarthy makes a big difference in his worth. It is possible to find a doll in the $600 price range, but a mint-in-box Charlie could bring $900.

During World War II Bergen and Charlie were performing for soldiers on an outpost in the Aleutian Islands of Alaska. One soldier in the audience was suffering from battle fatigue and amnesia. He had been uncommunicative for weeks. The doctors could not reach him. But as Bergen and Charlie went at it, the soldier came to and smiled. He recognized Charlie's voice. He eventually made a full recovery.

Scarlett O'Hara

THE FIRST SCARLETT DOLL stepped right out of the book. After reading Margaret Mitchell's monumental novel *Gone With the Wind*, Beatrice Alexander, founder of the Alexander Doll Company, took one of her composition Tiny Betty dolls, dressed her in a yellow organdy ruffled gown and a straw hat adorned with velvet flowers, and called her "Scarlett."

Two years later David O. Selznick released his film *Gone With the Wind*, and in 1937 Alexander got exclusive rights from Selznick and MGM to produce and market Scarlett O'Hara dolls. Shortly afterward, toy and department stores were inundated with miniature Southern belles. The dolls came in many sizes and all of them, except the first Scarlett doll, had the same round eyes, beautiful lips, and cloud of black hair almost encircling their faces. In Scarlett's case, however, the clothes made the doll. Alexander and her staff created hundreds of remarkable outfits for Scarlett using remnants of fine fabrics collected from New York City's garment district.

Like the actresses who played the Southern ladies in the film, the Scarlett doll was always perfectly dressed. Her wide-skirted gowns were trimmed with lace, ribbons, and rosettes; her pantaloons were trimmed with lace; and a hat or bonnet matched each dress. This doll, eleven inches tall and "The Only Authentic" Scarlett O'Hara doll, according to a 1939 newspaper advertisement, cost seven dollars.

The first great era in Alexander Scarlett dolls ended in 1943. A decade passed before the company introduced another Scarlett O'Hara. By that time, the great Southern belle had joined the modern postwar world: she was made of plastic.

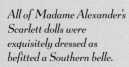

All of Madame Alexander's Scarlett dolls were exquisitely dressed as befitted a Southern belle.

Melanie

MELANIE, THE OTHER HEROINE IN *Gone With the Wind*, first appeared as a Madame Alexander doll in 1956. As a doll, Melanie never achieved anywhere near the popularity of Scarlett. As in the book and the movie, Scarlett got top billing; Melanie was best supporting doll.

Melanie was a much-loved character, however, and over the years there have been at least seven Melanie dolls of various sizes and types of faces. According to collectors of Alexander dolls and those who collect *Gone With the Wind* memorabilia, the Melanies produced in 1970 are the most striking. One Melanie from that year is a twenty-one-inch brunette with brown eyes and long eyelashes made of real hair. She is dressed like a proper antebellum belle in a white dress of ruffled tiers trimmed with white lace and red satin ribbons. A wide, white straw hat sits on her dark brown hair, which is parted in the middle and pulled to the sides in two clusters of four curls, like Olivia de Havilland's in the movie. To top it all off, Melanie wears a tiny cameo necklace.

Melanie appears as a blonde in the Portrait Miniature series, also produced in 1970. This doll was eleven inches tall and has the Cissette "adult" body. Her hair is parted in the middle and tied back with yellow bows. Her gown is yellow organdy with eight rows of lace cascading down the skirt. And she's wearing gold high-heeled sandals.

Madame Alexander created two versions of Melanie. One was blond; the other, a brunette.

Dy-Dee Baby

THE DY-DEE BABY WAS TOUTED as "The Almost Human Doll." Her chief attraction was her ability to "wet!"

The child simply inserted the nipple of the water-filled Dy-Dee nursing bottle into the doll's open rosebud mouth, let her drink an ounce or so, and, in due course, the doll would wet her diaper. Then the little girl could undertake that fundamental task of parenthood and change the baby.

Here's how it worked: Inside the doll a rubber tube led from the mouth to an opening in the hips. Dy-Dee had a patented valve in her works that prevented water from leaking out as soon as she took a drink. In other words, it took a fairly realistic amount of time for the contents of the bottle to reach her diapers.

Dy-Dee was introduced in 1934. She was designed for Effanbee by Bernard Lipfert, who was also responsible for Bye-Lo Baby, Patsy, Toni, and the Shirley Temple doll.

Dy-Dee, although a toy, had an important mission. Accompanying each doll was a booklet, an owner's manual written by "Aunt Patsy." Included was a note to the parent that stated, "It is our sincere belief that Mother-Love can best be engendered in the hearts of little girls during their tender, formative years. It is in this spirit that we dedicate the Dy-Dee Baby to every little girl who has the capacity for that greatest of all emotions—Mother-Love."

Dy-Dee came in about six sizes. Each size had its own name, a variation of Dy-Dee. There was nine-inch Dy-Dee Wee, eleven-inch Dy-Dee-ette, thirteen-inch Dy-Dee-Kin, and Dy-Dee Baby, the more or less standard, at fifteen inches long. Finally, there was Dy-Dee-Lou, who was a lifelike twenty inches.

Dy-Dee could be bought separately or with a wide variety of accessories, trunks, layettes, and carrying cases. Dy-Dee's Complete Layette included a nursery dress, a sleeper, cotton swabs (to clean Dy-Dee's flexible rubber ears and "the cutest turned-up nose with nostrils that are open and need cleaning, too"), baby powder, soap,

In addition to paraphernalia for drinking water and blowing bubbles, Dy-Dee Baby also came with an owner's manual written by "Aunt Patsy."

towels, a baby blanket, and three nursing bottles. Also available were Dy-Dee Sleeping Garments, Flannel Zipper Buntings, and Rubber Panties. Clothes could easily be made for Dy-Dee, too. In the 1930s McCalls had patterns just for Dy-Dee dolls.

Since Dy-Dee was almost human, tending her was almost a full-time job. She could drink from her bottle, of course, and was the only doll of her day that was able to drink sitting or lying down. She could also drink from a spoon. Diapering Dy-Dee was a demanding chore. According to the booklet that accompanied her, her diapers "may need two or three changes after each feeding" and "her little mother should be ever watchful for her baby's comfort."

Dy-Dee could be bathed safely because she had "air-tight joints." Aunt Patsy advised, "Her ears should be cleaned once a day." You could keep Dy-Dee's eyes open or closed with a gentle twist of her head. "Remember . . . you must never twist Dy-Dee's head too far sideways," warned Aunt Patsy, "because that would hurt her." You could powder her, too, making her ready for a "jolly romp."

A jolly romp for Dy-Dee was blowing bubbles. "It is so simple," Aunt Patsy exclaimed. "Just dip the bubble pipe"—another one of Dy-Dee's accessories—"in a bowl of soapy suds and place the nippled stem of the pipe in the doll's mouth." Then press the doll's tummy and "My, what beautiful soap bubbles Dy-Dee blows!"

Dy-Dee was so lifelike, as dolls go, that she was promoted as "the perfect doll for prenatal education used by nursing classes, by Red Cross, Boards of Education, and Child Care organizations the World Over."

After World War II, Dy-Dee had a crier-pacifier. With the pacifier in her mouth, Dy-Dee could cry. By the late 1940s and early 1950s, plastic had replaced hard rubber as the stuff dolls were made of. Dy-Dee made the change, but kept her flexible rubber ears. Like most other play dolls, she became vinyl in the next decade. Black Dy-Dee appeared in the late 1960s. Montgomery Ward, observing its hundredth anniversary in 1973, sold a seventeen-inch all-vinyl Dy-Dee.

Betsy Wetsy

AT A COCKTAIL PARTY IN 1955, the young mother of two children cornered the president of Ideal Toy Corporation. She explained that she had a baby and a preschooler at home. The little girl was frustrated and felt left out because of the time her mother had to spend with the baby.

"Doesn't anyone make a realistic baby doll that could actually do something that real babies can do?" the mother asked. She felt that the situation would be better if her daughter could look after a baby doll while she took care of the baby.

In 1937 Ideal had made such a doll of composition and rubber. As a result of that cocktail party conversation eighteen years later, the company reissued Betsy Wetsy, a vinyl drink-and-wet baby who could also be dunked in the bath and have her hair shampooed.

Betsy Wetsy came in a variety of sizes, from nine inches (Baby Betsy Wetsy) to twenty-four inches. Some had hair with more than a thousand strands rooted in the scalp; others had molded hair. Betsy's eyes were wide and blue. And, wet or dry, she had polished apple cheeks and a contented expression.

Betsy Wetsy usually came with a layette, and perhaps a bonnet. To keep her clean a little girl might be able to persuade her mother to buy a Betsy Wetsy bathtub. Then she and her mother could work side by side.

First made in 1937, Betsy Wetsy was successfully reintroduced to a new generation eighteen years later.

Ginny

GINNY, ALTHOUGH A QUINTESSENTIALLY CUTE CHILD fashion doll, was one tough girl. You could play with Ginny all day—in the house, down the stairs, outside in the park—and, for festive occasions, dress her in one of her innumerable elaborate outfits. One of the first eight-inch dolls, and therefore extremely portable, Ginny was just about ideal for play. She was a companion for generations of little girls.

The Ginny story dates to 1922 when Jennie Graves, thirty-year-old mother of three, opened the Vogue Doll Shoppe. Mrs. Graves bought German bisque dolls and sold them dressed in the magnificent outfits she made. In the 1950s, one of her daughters, Virginia Graves Carlson, took over creative responsibility and gave the doll her own name.

Jennie Graves had begun producing the dolls in composition during the late 1930s, and from the first, Vogue dolls had a reputation of near indestructibility. Porcelain dolls were fragile, and parents often limited play to "special occasions." The Vogue dolls, which despite their many names have become known as Ginny, were made for play.

Ginny's reputation for being able to take anything a child dished out rose higher when plastic was seized upon after World War II as the medium of choice by the doll industry. Plastic simply enhanced Ginny's capability to go anywhere and do anything. It was a good thing, too, because judging from the number and variety of the doll's accessories, Ginny could be anyone, including a kindergarten moppet, a cowgirl, a ballerina, and even a regally costumed queen. Ginny had travel packages, skiing outfits, a gym set, a hospital room, and her "own custom designed wardrobe trunk." There were earmuffs, jewelry, and eyeglasses for her. Ginny even had her own designer bed linen.

Ginny was affordable, and while other dolls were sold in specialty shops or only in the finer department stores, Ginny was available almost everywhere, from doll shops to corner drugstores.

Ginny's career as an all-around, all-purpose child fashion doll that a youngster could actually have fun with has lasted for more than fifty years. She and lots of her outfits are still being sold today. The older versions of Ginny are now collectibles, evocative symbols of childhood for thousands of women.

One of the first eight-inch dolls, Ginny, who is still being made today, has an enormous number of outfits and accessories.

Dewees Cochran Dolls

*Dewees Cochran dolls
looked extremely realistic.
This doll has one of the six
basic head shapes of the
Look-Alike dolls, four of
which were produced
by Effanbee.*

THE DOLLS THAT DEWEES COCHRAN MADE were subtly distinctive, different from other dolls. Even today, many years later, they still stand out.

Ella Dewees (pronounced D'wees) Cochran was born in Dallas, Texas, and raised in Philadelphia. In the 1920s she gained notice as a painter and sculptor in America and abroad. After the stock market crash of 1929 and during the ensuing Depression people were investing in neither paintings nor sculpture, so she decided to try her hand at making dolls.

Cochran's first dolls were long-legged black cloth characters she called Topsy and Turvey. Then she made bodies for German china heads and dressed the dolls in Early American costumes. She sold them in New York to Saks Fifth Avenue and F.A.O. Schwarz for Christmas 1934. A buyer at Saks offered her valuable advice: whimsy was out of fashion, realism was in.

It was then that Cochran began making her Portrait Dolls. She carved the heads from wood. The bodies were cloth. The dolls could be played with by little girls or they could be treasured by collectors. The idea and the dolls caught on immediately. Among her first orders were dolls for Irving Berlin's two daughters.

Carving the heads from balsa wood was time-consuming and limited her production, so Cochran began to work in plastic wood. This enabled her to cast the limbs and the basic head shapes and personalize each one for a portrait.

Experimentation and constant refinement led her to another stage and innovation in doll making. As she sculpted heads, and subsequently looked at thousands of photographs of children at the New York Public Library, she became aware of six basic types of faces of American children. She went to Effanbee with a new concept, and in 1936 signed a three-year contract to make her American Children series. The dolls, twenty-one inches tall, were made of composition. In the three years, about fifty thousand American Children dolls were produced.

It was also during the 1930s that Cochran introduced her Look-Alike line of dolls. They were made to order to look like the little girls that owned them. They were priced from forty-five to sixty-four dollars.

The dolls brought Cochran fame. Articles about them and her innovative methods appeared in national newspapers and magazines, and on radio programs. Paramount Pictures produced three documentary shorts about Dewees Cochran, and Cochran appeared with one of her Look-Alike dolls on the cover of the April 3, 1939, issue of *Life* magazine.

World War II closed down Cochran's doll making, but after the war she used materials that had been developed from wartime technology. Early in the 1950s she created a new line of Portrait Dolls. Then, during a bout of melancholia after the Christmas season, Cochran made a doll of a five-year-old child she named Susan Stormalong, or Stormy. The following three years, Cochran made Stormy at eleven, sixteen, and twenty years of age. That turned into another commercial line, Grow-Ups, costing from twenty-five to thirty-five dollars for each doll.

Cochran moved to California in 1960 and made dolls in her workshop for another twenty years. She died in 1991 at the age of ninety-nine. She left no surviving relatives—just dolls for generations of children to play with and love, in homes all over the country.

Little Lady

LITTLE LADY MADE HER APPEARANCE toward the end of the 1930s. Manufactured by Effanbee, she was an Anne Shirley doll with a new name. Little Lady was made of composition and came in a range of sizes, from about fifteen inches to twenty-nine inches tall. Her hands were particularly graceful; they had separate fingers and had been sculpted by the doll maker Dewees Cochran. In 1938 Little Lady had Magic Hands, which had magnets in the palms to allow her to hold such things as a parasol.

In the 1940s, her most popular decade, Little Lady came in a suitcase along with a nineteen-piece wardrobe. She was identified as Party Girl, Pedal Pusher, or Drum Majorette; each persona came with appropriate outfits.

By 1950, the Anne Shirley connection was severed, but Little Lady survived. She looked younger, chubbier, and less classic. She was now made of plastic. The Little Lady of 1954 was fifteen inches tall, all vinyl and jointed. She wore a long-sleeved dress and an organdy pinafore. The package in which she came was filled with Little Lady Toiletries, including shampoo, talcum powder, a powder puff, a comb, mirror, curlers, and perfume.

In 1960, Little Lady was a bride. Twenty inches tall, she was dressed in a long embroidered nylon gown. She had a bridal bouquet, pearl earrings, and a sparkling engagement ring.

The early Little Lady dolls, like the inset above, had molded, painted hair. The later dolls had real hair. They were all beautifully dressed.

Little Women

THREE YEARS AFTER THE CIVIL WAR ENDED, Louisa May Alcott published a novel inspired by her own family's experiences. Since then, girls have been making Alcott's four heroines— Meg, Jo, Beth, and Amy—members of their own families.

Paper dolls of the four sisters appeared in women's magazines soon after the turn of the century. The first three-dimensional dolls were produced a little later during the Broadway run of a play based on the novel. A new edition of the novel, published in the 1920s and timed with the release of the silent film *Little Women*, resulted in a new set of dolls influenced by Jessie Willcox Smith's illustrations for the book.

The doll maker Madame Alexander, herself the eldest of four sisters, loved Alcott's novel. Her first Little Women dolls were made of cloth, had painted faces, and were dressed in period costumes. Another film version of *Little Women* was made in 1933, this time with sound. In its wake, Alexander came out with a series of little Little Women; these March sisters were only seven inches tall.

Madame Alexander was not the only doll maker producing Little Women. In the 1940s one set of dolls included Marmee. This was the Godey's March family, produced by doll maker Ruth Gibbs, who made Godey's Lady Book Dolls.

In 1949, the novel was again made into a movie, with June Allyson as Jo, Elizabeth Taylor in a blond wig as Amy, and Peter Lawford as Laurie. Alexander came out with another March family, now including Marmee. This line of Little Women was in circulation—with minor changes and new costumes every year—until the mid-1950s.

Alcott's *Little Women*, now well over a century old, remains refreshing and engaging. The most recent cinematic adaptation of the novel, the much praised 1995 film starring Wynona Ryder, heralded new dolls based on the March sisters. These were produced by a number of manufacturers, including Wendy Lawton, Ashton-Drake, and, of course, the Madame Alexander Doll Company.

These eight-inch Little Women by Madame Alexander were part of the display on the Bicentennial Freedom Train that toured the United States in 1976.

1940–1949

THE EARLY 1940S IS ETCHED IN AMERICAN HISTORY as the period of World War II. The United States had avoided becoming embroiled in the conflict in Europe and ignored the problems in the East until Japan's fateful air attack on Pearl Harbor on December 7, 1941. In two hours the Navy lost three times as many men as in World War I and the Spanish-American War combined. Suddenly there was the realization that there was no escape from this terrible conflagration.

In contrast to the obvious conflict-related tragedies, the war was a boon to the economy. It brought prosperity to millions. It was also the catalyst for great progress in technology and medicine. Atomic energy, commercial television, radar, penicillin, and synthetic fabrics are only a few of the many examples. Because of the shortage of manpower, women flooded into the workplace. In many cases they took over jobs in traditional male areas. It is recorded, for example, that two out of every five workers in ammunition plants were women.

The movies still provided the favored form of escapism, although the plots, even of such classics as *Casablanca*, frequently centered on the war, which was usually highly romanticized. Radio brought entertainment into everyone's living room and became an important source of information and entertainment. President Roosevelt broadcast his fireside chats to a huge audience. The banter of Jack Benny, Red Skelton, and Bob Hope kept people laughing, as did shows like

Fibber McGee and Molly. Frank Sinatra was the popular singer and teenagers' idol of the day.

When the war ended in 1945, women were encouraged to go back to homemaking and let the men reclaim their jobs in offices and factories. A more affluent lifestyle became widespread. Fashions were glamorous again. Paris was once more the center of fashion and Dior became a household name. The reading public was shocked by the first Kinsey report that disclosed the sexual behavior of the human male and was delighted with Dr. Spock's revolutionary theories on raising children.

The doll industry thrived, too. During the war the technology for working with plastic had been greatly advanced, and in the early postwar era plastic became an obvious and popular material for many other products, including toys. (In 1940 a doll had been made of hard plastic, but was discontinued because of wartime restrictions.) Almost immediately after the war more than eighty-four companies began to make dolls molded in hard plastic. Foremost among them were the Alexander Doll Company, Effanbee, American Character, and Ideal.

Dolls were inspired by comic strip characters, by such celebrities as Margaret O'Brien, and, toward the end of the decade, by stars of the new medium—television. The red-haired Howdy Doody, for example, became a doll that appealed to boys and girls.

Cinderella

There have been many Cinderella dolls. This eleven-inch vinyl beauty was made by Effanbee.

CINDERELLA IS OLDER THAN SHE LOOKS. Her story is, perhaps, the best-known folktale in the world. There are said to be more than five hundred versions of the story in Europe alone. It is believed that the original Cinderella story came from China in about the ninth century A.D. But it was Charles Perrault, the seventeenth-century French writer, who wrote the best-known literary version of the tale. Over the years, Cinderella has appeared in many guises, from the heroine of a comic opera by Rossini to the star of the animated musical made by Walt Disney's studio in 1950 and re-released to a new generation forty-five years later.

As early as the mid nineteenth century, when women's magazines began to feature pages of cutout dolls, Cinderella was a prominent character. When American magazines started publishing paper dolls, Cinderella was the only folktale character to appear. Since that time other fairy tales and mythological characters have had their day as paper dolls, but Cinderella seems to be a consistent attraction.

The Cinderella Sitting Doll, designed by a Mrs. Irene Wilkinson Gibson somewhere around the 1860s, might be the earliest Cinderella doll. Cinderella with a "French" bisque head, sleep eyes, open mouth revealing teeth, and a kid body, was advertised in 1898 by W. A. Cissna & Company. Cinderella seems to have also made an appearance as a German jointed doll in 1898 and as an American rag doll in 1906. About four years later, the Naphtha Soap Powder company came out with a coupon doll called Cinderella. She had a bisque head, a sewed curly wig, sleep eyes, and an open mouth with teeth. This doll, available in sizes of nineteen, twenty-one, and twenty-six inches, was dressed in satin.

After World War II, as toy and doll companies began gearing up for what many collectors refer to as "the golden age of dolls," Cinderella appeared as a fourteen-inch hard-plastic princess, dressed in a flouncy gown. Her Prince Charming (you might have received them as a pair; no doubt Effanbee wanted you to buy both of them) wore a pink satin tunic, long white stockings, black slippers, a white cape, and a ridiculous-looking hat. No self-respecting prince would be caught dead in that get-up, but he was "charming" and in one hand he held a glass—really plastic—slipper.

At the same time, the Madame Alexander Doll Company came out with Cinderella dolls. Those hard-plastic dolls looked more like the Disney adaptation of the character. There were two Alexander versions. One was the poor Cinderella, dressed in ragged clothing. The other was the enchanting young woman who emerged after the fairy godmother had worked her magic. Also available from Alexander was a prince.

Since the 1950s, there have been many Cinderella dolls of all kinds. In 1965, a Horsman version had interchangeable poor and rich heads and matching costumes. Barbie appeared as Cinderella with both rags and riches costumes. Charmin' Chatty, Mattel's talking doll of the 1960s, also portrayed Cinderella. She came with a patched burlap smock and a mop, as well as a dress of pink satin, matching satin cape, a wand, and a pair of clear plastic slippers. Cinderella has been an ideal subject for manufactured and homemade topsy-turvy dolls: one end is the cinder wench, the other a beautiful princess. If you visited one of Disney's parks in the late 1970s, you might have acquired the doll that resulted from Effanbee's collaboration with Disney artists. One of a series that included Snow White and Sleeping Beauty, this doll had a booklet of scenes from the movie attached to her wrist. The two companies collaborated again in the 1980s. This Cinderella, unlike the previous one, was available both in the parks and in retail stores. In the mid-eighties, Vogue's Ginny, reissued by Meritus Industries, appeared as a limited-edition Cinderella. This doll was decked out in quasi-historical French style. Recently, Disney and the Madame Alexander Doll Company joined forces to issue a limited edition of Cinderella, primarily for collectors.

But you don't have to be a collector to bring home Cinderella. In just about every toy store, there are Cinderella dolls of sundry manufacturers and styles. Cinderella might date back to the ninth century, but she can still enchant young girls who play with dolls and believe in fairy tales.

Collector's Note

Effanbee's Cinderella is listed in current price guides at $400, and Madame Alexander's Cinderella between $400 and $700 depending on the face and condition.

Trudy

TRUDY WAS "3 DOLLS IN ONE." There was "nothing else like it." Indeed, advertisements went so far as to claim she was "The Most Amazing Doll Creation in a Decade."

Trudy, a three-faced doll, appeared in stores in 1946. All you had to do to change her face was turn a knob on top of her head. The faces not on view were hidden in her bonnet. Her three faces were registered as "Sleepy, Weepy, and Smiley."

Made of composition with molded and painted features, Trudy came in five versions, each dressed in a distinctive costume. The first Trudy was fourteen inches tall and wore a pink and blue sleeping outfit. Number two, who was the same size, wore a print party dress and bonnet. Third was Big Sister Trudy, who wore a pink party frock with matching panties and bonnet and was about twenty inches tall. Trudy number four was also fourteen inches, but evidently was not as popular as the others, since only scant information about this doll exists. The fifth Trudy, also fourteen inches, was dressed in a felt outfit and came with a handbag "ready for a shopping spree or a workout in a sandbox."

Designed by Elsie Gilbert for Three-In-One Doll Corporation of New York, Trudy was one of the last mass-produced composition dolls made for the mainstream market; plastic replaced just about all other manufacturing materials.

Trudy wasn't the first multiple-faced doll. In 1866, Dominico Checkeni had obtained a patent for a four-faced doll. Doll makers in France and Germany experimented with designs and produced multiple-faced dolls on and off during the nineteenth century.

In a 1913 issue of *Playthings*, the major magazine for the toy industry, there are several references to two-faced and three-faced dolls. Some had different expressions; others had one white face and one African-American face. Multiple-headed or multiple-faced dolls were made of most materials. The winner, judging just by the numbers, has to be a celluloid doll with five screw-on heads—three girls, a boy, and a cat.

Trudy No. 1 was adorable in her sleeping outfit. Here she is wide awake. Her crying and sleeping faces are shown above.

Collector's Note

A "mint"
Hedda-Get-Bedda,
that is to say, a doll in
pristine condition,
with the original box
and all her little
accessories, is worth
about $125 to
collectors.

Hedda-Get-Bedda

One of the most popular three-faced dolls was Hedda-Get-Bedda. A member of the Whimsies produced by American Character in 1960–61, Hedda was about twenty inches tall and had a vinyl head and a one-piece stuffed body.

Hedda's faces were, in no particular order, happy, sick, and sleeping. The happy face had bright painted eyes, a nubble of a nose, and a closed-mouth smile. By turning the pom-pom on top of her little cap, another face appeared. The under-the-weather face had droopy eyelids, an open weak mouth, and spots scattered over her cheeks, nose, and forehead. Hedda came with a play thermometer, a spoon, and a bottle of play medicine. She was dressed in a nightgown when you got her, the outfit conveying that this doll should be in bed.

After you took her temperature and dispensed medical advice ("Stay in bed, drink plenty of liquids, take your medicine . . .") you turned her knob to the third face. This face wore a sleeping, contented expression; her eyes were closed, her mouth turned in a slightly askew smile. Hedda-Get-Bedda had made another complete recovery.

Ideal Novelty and Toy Company also made a composition doll with three faces—sleepy, weepy, and smiling—in 1946. As with Trudy, the faces were rotated by turning a knob on top of the head. This doll was named Big Sister. Multiple-faced dolls were not new to Ideal. In 1916 Ideal had produced Baby Bi-Face, a two-headed doll, and in 1923 the company produced a three-headed doll named Snoozie Smiles.

Nevertheless, for her time Trudy was a remarkable and, despite the somewhat unsettling existence of her three faces, engaging doll.

According to published documents, Trudy was produced until at least 1947. That year, a Trudy cutout paper-doll set hit the market. She was "Queen of the Paper Doll World." Carried in such stores as Bloomingdale's, Macy's, and Kresge, she was the same doll as the original Trudy, only in paper.

Sparkle Plenty

SPARKLE PLENTY, THE CHILD OF GRAVEL GERTIE and B.O. Plenty, was born and made her first public appearance in the Dick Tracy comic strip on June 1, 1947. Excitement and suspense had been building for weeks. So had a kind of morbid amusement: how ugly would Gravel Gertie's and B.O. Plenty's baby be? Most bets were in favor of a boy. Chester Gould, Dick Tracy's creator, fooled everyone. The baby girl was as cute as Gould could draw her.

Gimbels, the New York City department store, had been tipped off to the event, and by July 28 they were well stocked with Sparkle Plenty dolls. Made by the Ideal Novelty and Toy Company, Baby Sparkle Plenty was fourteen inches tall, cost six dollars, and was dressed in a diaper and a flannel kimono. Her head was made of a substance called Celanese cellulosic plastic, touted for its "unbreakable toughness and high quality." The rest of her was made of "Magic Skin." She had blue eyes, long black eyelashes, and, like her comic strip double, long, wavy blond hair. The doll was chubbier, more compact, and even cuter in three dimensions than she was in the funny pages.

Gimbels did heavy promotion. To buy a doll, people fought their way through crowds of other Dick Tracy fans and their daughters. In a few months three sizes of Sparkle Plenty were being made and it was estimated that more than seven million children wanted Sparkle Plenty that first Christmas. In a clever piece of product promotion, the Sparkle Plenty doll appeared in the Dick Tracy comic strip; inside the doll's torso was a radio transmitter that helped the forces of Law and Order prevail.

The next year, Sparkle Plenty had a jointed rubber body. She could hold a bottle or suck her thumb. She was equipped with an internal mechanism that enabled her to cry and coo, and when squeezed, she seemed to breathe. That same mechanism made it possible for Sparkle Plenty to burp after her bottle. She also had plumbing that made her wet.

Sparkle Plenty's body was made of a substance that disintegrated with the passage of time. Few of these early Magic Skin dolls have survived.

Bonnie Braids

Collector's Note

Bonnie Braids sells today for $150 to $200, and twice that if she is still in her original comic strip box.

DICK TRACY'S ENGAGEMENT TO TESS TRUEHEART lasted for eighteen years. He asked her to marry him in the second daily strip, but they didn't get around to walking down the aisle until Christmas 1949. Bonnie Braids was delivered in a police car on May 14, 1951. She was named by a nurse and, though Dick Tracy hated it ("Bonnie Braids, Phooey!"), the name stuck.

Little girls liked the name—and the doll Ideal brought out the same year. To promote the new doll someone at Ideal persuaded the Los Angeles police (the New York police refused) to rush the doll to downtown department stores, sirens grabbing attention. After all, the comic strip baby had been born in a police cruiser. Back in New York City, Ideal's publicity representative dressed like a nurse and pushed the doll in a carriage up Fifth Avenue to the Central Park Zoo. Attached to the carriage was a banner that proclaimed, "Nobody But Nobody But Gimbel's has Bonnie Braids."

During the summer of 1951, Ideal was producing seven thousand Bonnie Braids a day. The doll was fourteen inches tall, with a vinyl head and a "Magic Skin" body. She had wide painted eyes, a pug nose, and a mouth molded to look open, revealing one lower tooth. Bonnie Braids was "the cutest little character ever to crawl out of a comic strip," according to one advertisement. Fresh from the store, the original doll came with a long organdy christening dress, a diaper, a long slip, and booties.

The next year, there was a new Bonnie Braids dressed as a toddler, with socks and shoes. In 1953 she was able to walk. This doll had a vinyl head, plastic body, molded yellow hair, and two braids made of synthetic hair. She wore a flowery dress and was available in fourteen- and sixteen-inch heights.

The 1953 version of Bonnie Braids was a toddler who was able to walk.

Terri Lee

*No matter what costume
they wore, all the Terri Lee
dolls had the same distinctive
little faces.*

THE TERRI LEE DOLL WAS MADE to play "that greatest of small girls' pastimes, dress up." Terri Lee was one of the most popular fashion dolls of her day. Her day began in 1946, when the dolls were first featured in the Montgomery Ward catalog, and faded in the late 1950s and early 1960s when the Terri Lee Company disintegrated because of claims of betrayal, lawsuits, and the factory's razing by arson. The final knell was the death in 1972 of Violet Gradwohl, the company's founder and driving force.

Terri Lee and the Terri Lee Company began in Violet's kitchen in Lincoln, Nebraska. The company grew rapidly. More than eight thousand dolls were sold the first year. Terri Lee's face was sculpted by Violet's cousin Maxine Runci and named after Violet's daughter. At first the doll was made of composition. When the supply of sawdust used in the composition mixture could not keep up with the demand for dolls, Violet called for a shipment of corn from the fields of Nebraska and used ground corn cobs for the construction material. Later Terri Lee dolls were made of the new "wonder" materials of plastic and vinyl.

The Terri Lee doll, regardless of whether she portrayed a ballerina or a nun, or whether she was called Bonnie Lou or Little Lady—or Jerri Lee, the male counterpart—had a distinctive look. Her head was large and her painted eyes were widely spaced. Her nose was snub and she had chubby cheeks and a pouty mouth.

But the main reason for Terri Lee's success was her wardrobe. Borrowing a strategy from Mary Hoyer, Violet Gradwohl encouraged her customers to make their own outfits with her specially designed patterns. Ready-made outfits were also available. They were made by hand, of fine fabrics, and included a majorette costume, a Scottish costume, the garden party dress, the Girl Scout and Brownie uniforms, a Calypso costume, and a cheerleader outfit.

Margaret O'Brien

Collector's Note

If you still have
your Margaret
O'Brien doll, you
could sell her for
somewhere between
$650 and $950,
depending on her size
and condition.

FROM THE TIME SHE WAS TWO YEARS OLD, Margaret O'Brien knew what she wanted to do in life. At that age, in 1939, Angela Maxine O'Brien was watching her aunt perform at the New York's Waldorf-Astoria Hotel. To everyone's surprise and delight she followed her aunt on stage and mimicked her every dance step. The story goes that as soon as she could talk, Maxine told her mother she wanted to be in the movies instead of watching them. When she was just seven years old she won a special miniature Oscar for "outstanding child actress of 1944" for her role in *Journey for Margaret.* Her most noteworthy later films were *The Canterville Ghost* and *Meet Me in St. Louis*, in which she played Tootie.

Margaret wasn't exactly popular with some of the actors from whom she stole scenes, but that aside, she was a very good child actress and many people considered her a "child marvel." As a doll, Margaret O'Brien was beloved by all and today is considered a star by doll collectors.

The Alexander Doll Company introduced the Margaret O'Brien doll in 1946. The first year she was composition. The following year, the doll was also available in hard plastic. She came in sizes of fourteen, eighteen, and twenty-one inches. She was fairly flexible, with joints at the neck, shoulders, and hips. Her blue glass eyes opened and closed. The Margaret O'Brien doll looked very much like Margaret O'Brien.

Madame Alexander's Margaret O'Brien doll looked very much like the popular child star.

Toni

IN 1949, JUST IN TIME FOR CHRISTMAS, the Ideal Novelty and Toy Company introduced Toni, named for the Gillette Company's home-permanent product. Ideal unleashed an aggressive promotion campaign linking the doll with the new Twentieth Century Fox movie *Oh, You Beautiful Doll,* starring June Haver. Toni dolls were given away as door prizes, theater lobbies were crowded with Toni doll displays, and before the lights dimmed on some Saturday morning shows, hairdressers demonstrated how to give the doll a Toni permanent. Gillette, of course, carried part of the campaign, and DuPont, the manufacturer of the doll's nylon hair, participated, too. The result of this salesmanship, and the peppy appeal of the doll herself, was that millions of Toni dolls were sold.

Toni came in many sizes. She could be dressed in about a hundred outfits, many of which were made of the new nylon "miracle" fibers. She was fairly expensive for her day and was definitely aimed at an upscale market.

In 1951, a dozen French fashion designers, including Jean Desses, Patou, Heim Paquin, Lafaurie, and Paquet, were recruited to design gowns for Toni. A group of beautifully dressed dolls then embarked on a tour of department stores across the country. It was perfect publicity and so successful that a dozen American designers, including such stars as Ann Fogarty, Oleg Cassini, and Ceil Chapman, were signed up. Their creations, introduced the following year at a charity fashion show

Toni, a pretty doll with a large wardrobe, had the distinction of being the first doll who could be given a home permanent.

Miss Curity

Miss Curity was one of several Ideal
dolls that had the Toni doll's head
and body. Miss Curity came
with a kit filled with Curity
products—cotton balls, gauze,
and adhesive bandages. A booklet
of first-aid instructions also
accompanied each doll. It's
always good to have a nurse
around the house.

at the Hotel Pierre in New York City, went on another tour.
These outfits were never mass-produced; they were
made solely to show off the dolls. It was possible,
however, to buy patterns of the outfits and make
them at home.

During Toni's heyday, her body was hard plastic,
jointed, and strung at the head, shoulders, and hips.
Consequently, each doll was sturdy, could be dressed
fairly easily, could be posed in many positions, and was
even capable of standing on her own. You could actually play
with this doll.

The Toni doll face and fundamental shape were so good
that they were reused for such other beloved dolls of that era as
Sara Ann, Miss Curity, Harriet Hubbard Ayer, and Betsy
McCall.

Honey

HONEY WAS ONE OF THE MANY DOLLS that came of age, so to speak, after World War II. She seemed to embody the optimism and relative opulence that most white Americans enjoyed during the 1950s. The Effanbee Doll Company added Honey ("A Sweet Child") to its line in 1948. She started out as a composition doll, and although two years later she was made of the new wonder material—plastic—her looks remained unchanged.

She had a chubby-cheeked, all-American wholesome face. In her first year, Honey had flirty eyes and wore fluffy dresses. By 1950, she was issued as a deluxe edition, again made of composition, accompanied by a trunk containing several outfits. The price was hefty—just under sixty dollars.

The first hard-plastic Honey was dressed in a majorette costume. The next year, however, saw Honey headed uptown—Effanbee decked her out in gowns by Elsa Schiaparelli, a renowned fashion designer of the day. Women's magazines took notice and gave the doll and her wardrobe rave reviews.

Honey learned to walk in 1953 and, accordingly, Effanbee changed her name to Honey Walker. How she was growing! She was now available in sizes up to twenty-five inches. She also had several new accessories, including a dog on a leash, a raincoat, and an umbrella.

Competition in the doll industry was at a high pitch during these years and no gimmick was considered too far-fetched. Honey's incarnation as the Tintair Doll was certainly a gimmick. Her platinum blond hair could now be tinted Glossy Chestnut or

Honey became the Tintair Doll, whose Dynel hair could be tinted to change her personality.

The Tintair Doll came with a hair coloring kit that contained two bottles of tints—Glossy Chestnut and Carrot Top.

Carrot Top simply by using the Safe Coloring Kit that came with her.

According to the advertisements, every little girl could play hairstylist with the Tintair Doll, who was said to be the first and only doll with three personalities. The "personalities" were her three hair colors: blond, redhead, and brunette. The doll came in three sizes and was made of plastic. Her hair, her most important feature, was made of Dynel, the new synthetic substance.

The Effanbee Tintair Doll Hair Coloring Kit contained a bottle of Carrot Top coloring and a bottle of Glossy Chestnut coloring (special blends of U.S. certified food colors), two Tintair Doll color applicators, a plastic dish, and plastic curlers. The young stylist was to ask her mother for a comb, an old towel, and safety pins.

The tinting was to be done in the bathroom sink, after the doll's clothes were removed and a towel was pinned around her shoulders. The new color was easy to brush on. It could then be washed out and the other color applied. It was suggested in the directions that the doll's hair color be changed frequently. Certainly, after tinting the doll's hair, her little stylist's clothing, and, probably, every surface in the bathroom, a refill hair coloring kit would be required.

By 1956, the little girls whom Honey had delighted in 1948 when she first appeared were in the throes of adolescence; they were growing up. And it seems as if the doll tried to accompany them. In 1957, Honey Walker had bending knees, high-heeled feet, and jointed ankles—all sure signs of burgeoning maturity in play dolls. Some versions of the doll had vinyl heads and rooted hair. But all these changes were in vain. Honey could not make it as a teenager. Other fashion dolls captured the market and Effanbee returned to making baby dolls. The next year, there was no mention of Honey in the Effanbee line.

Howdy Doody

HOWDY DOODY TIME LASTED FOR THIRTEEN YEARS. That's 2,543 groundbreaking television shows, and the program created a bonanza of merchandise. It all began in 1947. A radio program called *The Triple B Ranch*, on New York's WEAF, introduced the character that over the years would amuse and teach a generation of children manners and goodwill while dispensing tips on spelling and personal cleanliness.

Bob Smith—Big Brother Bob—the host of the radio show, was the voice of a character named Elmer, whose "Howdy Doody" greeting caught on with the young audience. Children clamored to see an actual Howdy Doody. So Smith and Vic

Howdy Doody came in different sizes and various costumes, but he always had forty-eight freckles, one for each state that was then in the Union.

Campbell, his collaborator, changed Elmer's name and decided to move him to television, the up-and-coming medium.

Frank Paris, a puppet maker, made the first Howdy Doody. When Paris learned that NBC was planning to have a toy version of the new TV star manufactured, he asked for a royalty. But the network decided that since Paris had been paid five hundred dollars outright he wasn't entitled to another nickel. Paris grabbed his puppet and stomped out into show business anecdotal history.

Bob Smith and NBC ad-libbed Howdy Doody's sudden disappearance and searched for a new Howdy Doody. Two animators from the Walt Disney Studio provided some sketches, which Smith and producers from the network combined to create a composite of the "new" star. In 1948 Velma Dawson, a Disney sculptor, made the Howdy Doody we all remember.

Howdy Doody, with his red hair, his Alfred E. Newman-like grin, and his forty-eight freckles (one for each state then in the Union), was just right for merchandising. There were Howdy Doody hand puppets, storybooks, coloring books, puzzles, craft sets, lampshades, dishes, masks, umbrellas, pail-and-shovel beach sets, bubble-bath concoctions, ukuleles, windup toys, shoe polish, and, naturally, dolls.

Almost as soon as Howdy Doody hit the airwaves, two companies nailed down licenses to manufacture Howdy Doodys. The Ideal Toy Corporation and the Effanbee Doll Company produced a variety of Howdy Doodys. The early dolls had composition heads and cloth bodies. A feature of some of the dolls was a string at the back of the neck, which, when pulled, would open and close Howdy Doody's mouth. Later, Howdy had a plastic head, blue or brown eyes that opened and closed, molded brown or red hair, a big nose, and stick-out ears. Both companies dressed Howdy Doody in pretty much the same outfit—dungarees, a long-sleeved plaid shirt, plastic cowboy boots, and a bandanna with his name on it, just in case the child did not recognize that famous face.

1950–1959

IN 1950 THE KOREAN WAR BEGAN. Terms like "cold war" and "Iron Curtain" peppered the vocabulary of radio and television newscasters. Senator Joseph McCarthy commandeered the airwaves with his "witch-hunts" for communists, looking for "a red under every bed."

The American public was, in most cases, secure at home. The 1950s was a period of economic prosperity. The postwar growth continued. In droves, middle-class families moved to the suburbs. Clusters of "prefab" houses encircled the cities. Commuting to work became the norm. Many people were sufficiently concerned about the cold war and the dangers of the atom bomb to construct fallout shelters in their backyards.

Unimagined technological advances were taking place; the polio vaccine was discovered and many drugs were produced from synthetics. A slogan of the day was "Better Living Through Chemistry." Civilians began to use computers. And in 1958 the Soviet Union launched *Sputnik*, the first satellite to orbit the earth, and the race to control outer space had begun.

Lucille Ball was the queen of television. James Bond was the movie hero of the day, and *Playboy* magazine (with Marilyn Monroe on the cover) invaded the newsstands. Elvis sang his way into the Top Ten charts, and in Cleveland, a disc jockey coined the term "Rock 'n' Roll" for the new sound in popular music. In 1955 Disneyland opened. Corvettes and T-Birds

were the hot cars. Queen Elizabeth's coronation in England was televised, and Grace Kelly, an American movie star, became a real princess.

In the toy world a golden age of doll making had begun. Children's television began to dominate the lives of youngsters, and affluent parents were able (and willing) to indulge their children by buying them many of the wondrous toys advertised on television—dolls that could walk, dolls with hair that could be combed, curled, and colored. The heroines of books like *Edith, the Lonely Doll* were the inspiration for dolls, as was the popular *McCall's* magazine paper doll, Betsy McCall.

In 1959, a new doll was displayed by Mattel at the New York Toy Fair. This doll, named Barbie, was to become a phenomenon. Although not particularly popular at first, Barbie became the eleven-and-a-half-inch alter ego of millions of young girls. Several dolls with adult figures, and fashionable clothes, like Dollikin, had become popular during the 1950s. When the voluptuous Barbie hit the scene, however, she devastated the competition. Within a couple of years, most of her rivals were discontinued. Barbie, Teenage Fashion Model, cost only three dollars retail. So girls could also own more than one and could buy extra costumes and accessories. It wasn't long before Barbie was on her way to making millions and millions of dollars for Mattel.

Betsy McCall

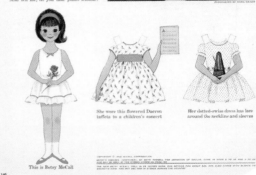

Betsy McCall was regularly featured in **McCall's** *magazine. This page from a 1962 issue has a little story about Betsy, a picture of the current doll at the piano, and a Betsy McCall paper doll.*

BETSY MCCALL WAS A CLASSICALLY CUTE all-American kid designed to sell the sewing patterns of *McCall's* magazine. She also became a popular playmate.

Betsy started as a paper doll in the May 1951 issue of *McCall's*, where she was featured standing shyly (dressed only in a slip), holding her own doll. There are four outfits on the page, along with her dachshund Nosy and Nosy's basket bed. It was easy to like Betsy McCall; her paper doll adventures were quiet, fun, homey, and safe. She was an adult's ideal child.

"Your Children Will Love to Play with Betsy McCall," declares a line on the magazine's cover. A fresh, squeaky clean, smiling girl named Peggy McGregor is the cover girl. In her chubby hands is the new paper doll. Before long Betsy McCall became so popular that *McCall's* made arrangements with Ideal to produce a plastic doll version.

Betsy made her debut as a three-dimensional doll in 1952. She was fourteen inches tall. Her head was vinyl; her body and limbs were plastic. She had sleep eyes and black hair. A McCall's pattern for an apron for the doll came with each Betsy.

The next year, Betsy shrank. Because of the sudden popularity of small dolls, *McCall's* issued a license to the American Character Doll Company for a seven-and-a-half-inch Betsy. This doll was made of hard plastic and was fully jointed. Her price matched her size; she was only two dollars and twenty-five cents. There were eighteen costumes for Betsy. Eventually there would be more than one hundred costumes to choose from.

Do you remember any of Betsy's outfits? One advertisement stated that it took designers and seamstresses at American Character an entire year to make Betsy's wardrobe. In that wardrobe were ensembles with names like Ballerina Coed, Sun 'n Sand, Town and Country (a black-and-white gingham dress and matching coat with red cotton lining, a snappy black beret, and black boots), April Showers, Holiday, and Cotillion, which consisted of a strapless evening gown in blue nylon net with blue tricot ruching, matching slip, panties, and shoes, all for three dollars.

As with the original fourteen-inch Ideal doll, there were many McCall's patterns for the "Slender Diminutive Doll's Instant

This fourteen-inch Betsy McCall is wearing an outfit called Schooldays. She was made in 1956 by the American Character Doll Company.

Wardrobe." There was one pattern for a ten-piece wardrobe, which included a bathrobe, pajamas, and a long lacy country dress, circa 1958. Patterns for girls' clothes that matched Betsy's outfits were also available from McCall's so that you and your doll could participate in the popular custom of dressing just like a brother or sister or friend.

By the time the 1960s rolled around, Betsy McCall was big. Indeed, she was almost as tall as a three-year-old. To compete with Ideal's Patti Playpal, who was the big girl, literally and in popularity, in the doll world at that time, in 1959 American Character came out with a thirty-six-inch Betsy. Her brother, Sandy, was two inches taller, and their relative, a cousin named Linda McCall, was thirty-six inches tall. Little girls or boys could now share their own clothes with their dolls.

In 1961, American Character issued yet another Betsy McCall. This one was about thirty inches tall. She had "Maxi-Flex movement" because of many strung joints. An advertisement boasted she could be posed in a thousand and one positions. This Betsy was available with five different hair colors and at least three different hairstyles. *McCall's* ran a series of advertisements featuring this Betsy in photographs that look quite lifelike. The following year American Character released its last Betsy. She was shorter, only twenty-two inches, but had the same flexible body as the previous doll.

Other toy and doll companies handled Betsy McCall during the rest of the 1960s and into the 1970s, but these dolls were teenagers without much charm, unable to compete in the same league with Barbie. Several companies produced "collectible" Betsy McCalls, but none of them were as collectible as the Betsys of the 1950s and 1960s. Then, in 1996, a redesigned Betsy McCall, both porcelain and vinyl, was introduced for collectors and children by the Robert Tonner Doll Company.

A slightly older, less sprightly version of the beloved doll was made by American Character in the early 1960s.

93

Cissy

CISSY WAS "THE DOLL WITH THE FIGURE OF A DEBUTANTE." Created in 1955 by the Alexander Doll Company, she had a hard-plastic head with saran hair. She was usually a blonde, but for a while she was a brunette and a redhead. She had a narrow waist and vinyl arms jointed at the elbows. Her feet were shaped for high-heeled shoes.

A tall doll, twenty and twenty-one inches, Cissy came in roles that required elaborate and glamorous costumes. She was dressed, for example, as Queen Elizabeth and as Scarlett O'Hara. Some stores had their own specially outfitted Cissys. In 1957, F.A.O. Schwarz, for example, featured a redheaded Cissy with blue eyes. She came with a round travel box that held an enormous trousseau. It included a pair of bright red mules, a red taffeta evening gown, a long-waisted dress of white organdy with a pleated sash held to the side with six rhinestones, a white taffeta petticoat (with three ruffles at the hem), a hot pink velvet coat, a pink nightgown, and lingerie, including white rayon panties, two lacy bras, a lacy girdle, a one-piece teddy, and two pairs of thigh-high nylon stockings.

More outfits could be added to Cissy's wardrobe by making her clothes at home. Simplicity produced patterns "all designed for the doll with the grown-up figure."

Cissy was created for clothes. You might well have received her for a gift. Standing in her wardrobe trunk she might have worn a navy blue taffeta dress, a white taffeta petticoat, panties, nylon stockings, and blue suede slippers with clear Lucite high heels.

This doll really knew how to dress.

Here is Cissy looking quite glamorous in a satin and lace teddy, a diaphanous negligee, nylon stockings, lace-trimmed mules, and satin and lace garters, one of which she seems to be thinking about donning.

Saucy Walker

Collector's Note

If you were prepared
to part with your
Saucy Walker from
the 1950s, a small one
(sixteen inches) would
fetch about $150.
The price for a large
(twenty-two-inch)
mint-in-box Saucy
would be about $400.

"DID YOU EVER SEE A DREAM WALKING?" an old song asked. Ideal Toy Corporation answered that question—and used that line in advertisements when it introduced Saucy Walker in 1951.

As her name indicates, Saucy Walker was a "walking" doll. You had to help. As you led the doll, rocking her on one leg until the other somehow stepped forward, Saucy Walker did her thing. One of the doll's arms could be raised only halfway, so you could take her hand. When Saucy Walker walked, her head turned from side to side and her eyes rolled.

Why was she called Saucy? She didn't fit Webster's first definition: "rude; impudent." The second definition sounds more like it: "pert; sprightly: as a saucy smile." Saucy Walker was a pleasant-looking, chubby child who looked like a well-fed three-year-old. She was sixteen or twenty-two inches tall. Her saran hair came in a variety of colors. Was yours a blonde, a brunette, or a redhead? Invariably, she wore bangs and braids with bows. There was a set of curlers attached to her name tag in case you wanted to do her hair. Saucy Walker's eyes looked to one side. Her mouth was open just enough to reveal two front teeth. And not only did she move, but when you picked her up she cried a long waaaahh. Her sound system was located in her chest.

Saucy Walker wasn't cheap for her time. The sixteen-inch doll cost just under ten dollars. The larger version cost just under sixteen dollars. The price did not dissuade customers. Saucy Walker was "the Walking Doll that Became a Runaway Bestseller," according to one advertisement. She was "the doll that does everything!—even breaks sales records!" Saucy Walker kept good company, if her advertisements are any indication. Piper Laurie, the ingenue in the Tony Curtis films of the 1950s, promoted the doll, and Dorothy Lamour co-starred with Saucy Walker in the Sears, Roebuck catalog.

Saucy turned her head from side to side and rolled her eyes when she walked. When she was picked up, she let out a loud cry. Here she is all ready for school, even with an apple for the teacher.

Alexander-Kins

ALEXANDER-KINS, INTRODUCED IN 1953, were probably made to be displayed rather than played with. Like almost all Alexander dolls, clothes were the reason for their creation. They were miniature mannequins showing off Madame Alexander's flair with designer fabrics.

The first Alexander-Kin was named Wendy Ann, after Beatrice Alexander's granddaughter. More characters followed: figures from literature like Peter Pan, the Little Women, and Hansel and Gretel and stock types like Little Southern Girl. Over the years, many others were added, including Apple Annie, Cheri, Curleylocks, Scarlett O'Hara, and Romeo and Juliet.

By 1954, the Alexander-Kins had a "walker" device. A few years later they had bending knees, which allowed them to sit on their specially made furniture. By the end of the decade, the most popular Alexander-Kin was Wendy (shortened from Wendy Ann). She was thematically packaged—Wendy Calls on a School Friend or Wendy Does the Mambo, for example—and dressed in appropriate outfits. As teenage fashion dolls gained favor, however, the little-girl looks of the Alexander-Kins and their diminutive size worked against their competing in that arena. And when Barbie stormed into the doll world, the teenage fashion doll market belonged to Mattel.

Alexander, however, was not easily stymied. She simply found a new niche, introducing the International Alexander-Kins in 1961. Dressed in costumes that represented nations around the world, the dolls became both collectibles and educational playthings. Then, in the middle of the 1960s, the Wendy-Kins appeared, featuring little-girl outfits. But by then little-girl dolls were passé; dolls had to be teenagers, with lots of outfits and boyfriends. Nevertheless, the Alexander-Kins are still with us. In recent years, they have been fairies, elves, and *Wizard of Oz* characters, and have portrayed such holiday themes as Mothers' Day, "I Love You" Valentine, and Easter Bonnet.

Fashions in the doll world come and go, but quality in small packages seems to endure.

*Only eight inches tall,
the Alexander-Kins were
dressed in adorable outfits.*

Dollikin

DOLLIKIN WAS "THE DOLL MIRACLE OF FLEXIBILITY." Made by Uneeda Toy Company in 1957, she had sixteen joints strung together so she could pose in just about any position; the copy on the box she came in stated, "Flexible joints to virtually copy all human poses." She was "The Completely New Idea!"

Like many dolls of her day, Dollikin was a fashion model. She was eighteen inches tall and looked a little older than a teenage doll. She had large eyes, a pouty mouth, and blushed cheeks. She was either a blonde, a brunette, or a redhead, and her hair was done in a variety of hairstyles.

Dollikin came in one of several outfits. She was dressed casually or in a nightlife party dress, as a dancer, a bride, or a young mother. To get a new outfit, you had to buy the doll who was wearing it. Dollikin's packaging was almost as eye-catching as she was. Through the cellophane you could see a "stage" on which, sitting demurely in one corner or reclining on a painted lawn chair, Dollikin displayed her flexibility. The boxes were decorated with sketches of a miniature figure—one assumed it was Dollikin—dancing, tumbling, doing some kind of aerobic exercise, golfing, playing tennis, and, since she was also a doll of glamour, posing in a chic outfit.

Dollikin was assigned specific roles that were illustrated on the package. Mommy Dollikin, for example, came with an eight-inch all-vinyl baby. The background artwork on the box showed a cartoony father and a goofy-looking dog posed next to a backyard barbecue grill. Miss Twist showed Dollikin following Chubby Checkers's exhortations.

Later, there was also Baby Dollikin, who was twenty-one inches long, a fairly flexible baby with eleven joints. Dollikin was around until the early 1970s. By that time she had shrunk to seven and a half inches.

One purported feature of Dollikin was her educational value. As was pointed out on her packaging, she was "A Model for Sewing and Sketches," but just in case that sounded a little too serious, it also added that Dollikin was "A Thrill Just to Play With."

Dollikin was extremely flexible and looked older than the teenage dolls of her day.

Jill, Jan, and Jeff

JILL, GINNY'S BIG SISTER, was the top teenage high-fashion glamour girl of her day. In her day everyone still liked Ike, watched Donna Reed on black-and-white television, and listened to Debbie Reynolds sing "Tammy" and Johnny Mathis sing "Chances Are." Elvis Presley was "All Shook Up."

Made by the Vogue Doll Company in 1957, Jill was ten and a half inches tall, slim, and had the obligatory high-heeled feet. She came with blond, brunette, or auburn hair, tied up in a ponytail or with a flip like Sandra Dee's, a hairstyle described as an "angel cut."

For the now small sum of three dollars, the basic Jill was dressed in black leotards or in a bra and girdle set. Eight dollars bought Jill fully dressed. Clothes were the reason Jill existed.

Her wardrobe was huge. She had everything from dungarees to flouncy prom formals. To judge from her outfits Jill seemed to be involved in almost every activity. She studied ballet, rode horses, ice-skated, skied, went to parties, spent time at the pool. And almost all her outfits had matching furs, hats, handbags, or jewelry. She even had her own custom furniture.

Like many other sisters of that long-ago world of elaborate fashion, Jill and Ginny often wore matching outfits. Another sister, Jan, who had a slightly more modern look, appeared in 1958, as did Jill's boyfriend, Jeff. He was half an inch taller and had enough clothes to escort Jill anywhere.

The next year, 1959, was the beginning of a mercilessly quick end for Jill. Barbie appeared on the scene and by 1962 Jill was history, only a memento of happy days.

Jeff, who was Jill's boyfriend, was half an inch taller and had almost as many outfits as she did.

98

Jill and Jan were Ginny's sisters and they could wear each other's clothes.
They are dressed here to go to a party, escorted by Jeff, who looks quite dapper.

Edith, the Lonely Doll

DARE WRIGHT, A WRITER AND PHOTOGRAPHER, immortalized Edith by making her the heroine of *The Lonely Doll* and many other children's books, including *Edith and Midnight, Edith and the Duckling,* and *A Gift From the Lonely Doll.* The books are illustrated with photographs of Edith and her friends, including Mr. Bear, engaged in charming, quiet adventures.

Dare Wright's "Edith" was made by the Italian doll maker Enrico Scavini. She was a typical creation of the Lenci company, founded by Scavini's wife, Elena, known as Lenci. The doll had a pressed felt head and blue-gray painted eyes. Her felt body and limbs were stuffed with cotton and she wore a pink-and-white gingham dress and hoop earrings. By the time the first book was published, however, this Edith was no longer available in the stores.

It was not until 1958 that there was an official Edith doll; she was made by the Alexander Doll Company. She did not look much like the Edith pictured in the books, although she was dressed in the pink-and-white dress and wore the hoop earrings. She was fifteen inches tall, with a hard-plastic body and a vinyl head. Her rooted blond hair was secured in a pony-tail and tied with a black velvet ribbon. She wore a wrist tag that read "Edith, the Lonely Doll" by Madame Alexander. A copy of the book came with each doll.

In 1985, Rothschild Doll Company of Massachusetts made a new Edith. Twenty-one inches tall, she was a fully jointed wool-felt doll and bore a fair likeness to the Lenci original. Her little face was handpainted and she had human hair. She came with her friend Mr. Bear, a cotton pillow, and a copy of *The Lonely Doll,* signed by Dare Wright. Unfortunately, this Edith was produced for only twelve months.

A new Edith is now being made by Martha and Kent Melton, doll makers who were granted the exclusive rights by Dare Wright to produce Edith dolls for five years. This Edith is made of felt with painted features, like the original doll, and she has the same look. Although this Edith is a limited edition, made primarily for collectors, there is talk of reproducing her in vinyl for distribution to stores across the country.

This Edith doll, made by Madame Alexander, did not look like the doll in the book, although she was dressed exactly the same way.

Sweet Sue

THE BROCHURE THAT ACCOMPANIED SWEET SUE stated that she was "the most glamorous doll in the world." And the girls who owned her certainly agreed.

Sweet Sue was ushered into stores in 1955 by the American Character Doll Company. She could be outfitted from head to pointed toes from an astonishing array of clothes including dirndl skirts, "Sunday Best" dresses, plaid pleated skirts (for school and around the office), bridal gowns, nightgowns, coats, and a huge choice of accessories. Her clothes, some of which were designed by master fashion designers, were available in choices of colors. Sweet Sue had the wardrobe many girls dreamed of having when they were finally "grown-up."

Sweet Sue was a flexible clothes tree. She could bend at the waist, assume fairly realistic dance poses, and with help she could even walk, so to speak, pivoting on one foot then the other, shifting her weight with each step. And she could clasp her hands.

This doll was hard plastic. Her eyes winked, and her hair could be curled with your curlers or, in a pinch, set with bobby pins. She was made in five sizes and cost from about nine dollars to twenty dollars.

Sweet Sue had a variety of second names, depending on the way she was dressed or her hairstyle. Perhaps you had a Sweet Sue Sophisticate, a Queen of Diamonds, or a Sweet Sue, Godey Lady.

Whatever her official name, or whatever you called her, she was the classiest and one of the most beloved fashion dolls around.

Until Barbie.

Little girls dressed Sweet Sue in the kind of dresses they dreamed of wearing themselves when they were grown up.

Baby Sue

Baby Sue was the infantile version of Sweet Sue. Made of vinyl, her body is stuffed with a substance that gives her weight, making her more realistic, particularly when she is hugged. She has wire rods inside her legs, enabling them to bend and hold a simple pose. You can tell by the baby's frilly dress that even at an early age, Sue was made for clothes.

Collector's Note

The size and condition of Sweet Sue are important. In excellent condition the doll would cost about $300.

Barbie

IN THE TIME IT TAKES YOU TO READ THIS SENTENCE, someone, somewhere, will buy a Barbie. Pause, take a breath, and another Barbie, perhaps two, will be sold.

Barbie is a doll and then some. She has been invested with cultural significance and psychological importance. The amount of press Barbie has generated during her thirty-seven years could fill several bookshelves. There are always books about the doll—some are glossy picture books filled with photographs, others are collectors' guides, and a few are "learned" studies—competing for space in the local bookstores.

She is almost continuously the focus of controversy. The Barbie image, claim her detractors, "is the airhead who consumes. She conditions children to be materialistic. She presents an unrealistic and potentially dangerous image of what women should look like." Two psychologists found that a young, healthy woman would have to be seven feet two inches tall, with five more inches out front, to have the same body proportions as Barbie. They arrived at the conclusion that a young man would have to be seven feet eight inches tall to look like Barbie's friend Ken.

But Barbie simply smiles at her critics. She is bigger than academia. This doll is a worldwide industry.

Perhaps, like other facets of popular culture, Barbie is best profiled by statistics and trivia.

❀ Barbie was named after the daughter of her creators, Ruth and Elliot Handler. Her full name is Barbie Millicent Roberts.

❀ She graduated from Willows High School.

❀ Barbie's astrological sign is Leo.

❀ Every day, at the Mattel Testing Laboratory, each Barbie is dropped headfirst, ten times, from a height of five feet. Each Barbie is also strapped into a machine that flexes her knees three hundred times. To be sure her makeup won't be less than perfect after a day at the beach, each doll is buried in and scrubbed with sand.

✿ The typical American girl (if there is such a creature) owns eight Barbies.

✿ Barbie is sold in more than one hundred countries around the world.

✿ According to some accounts, more than seven hundred million Barbies have been sold since 1959.

✿ Twenty million—give or take a million—Barbie outfits are sold annually. About one hundred and twenty new outfits are designed for Barbie each year.

✿ More than a billion outfits have been sold since 1959.

✿ Barbie has more than a billion pairs of shoes.

✿ More than a million yards of fabric have gone into the manufacture of the outfits of Barbie and her friends.

✿ During the past thirty or so years, Barbie has had as pets fifteen dogs, nine horses, a parrot, three cats, a lion cub, a giraffe, a zebra, and other assorted animals.

✿ The best-selling Barbie ever is the Totally Hair Barbie, first introduced in 1992. More than ten million of them were sold, generating more than one hundred million dollars.

✿ First editions of the original Barbies (Number Ones) can fetch as much as two thousand dollars on the doll and collectibles market. And while blondes may have more fun, first-run brunette Barbies are more valuable.

All this began with a German doll created to look like a cartoon character named Bild Lilli. Ruth Handler, who, with her husband, Elliot, owned Mattel (the toy company that made Mr. Potato Head), had long wanted to produce a fashion doll with an adult figure. In 1957, on a trip to Europe, she came across Bild Lilli. The doll, with some minor alterations, had the look she was seeking.

Over the years, Barbie has appeared in so many outfits that, if they were human-size, her wardrobe could clothe entire countries. Her first appearance was in the black-and-white-striped bathing suit.

Once home, she convinced the design department at Mattel that such a doll, marketed properly, could sell in the United States. After a design had been worked out, Mattel took another step, one that was unusual in 1957, and contracted with a Japanese firm to produce the doll.

The Barbie doll was introduced to the toy industry—and the world—in 1959 at the International Toy Fair in New York City. At first the doll, which cost three dollars, received a lukewarm response. But advertisements on television and canny marketing displays at stores helped push Barbie into the hands of young girls.

Soon Barbie was booming.

By 1963, *Life* magazine stated that Barbie was "the Most Popular Girl in Town." Almost from the first, many, many girls were able to act out their adolescent, if largely materialistic, fantasies through this buxom eleven and a half inches of vinyl.

The truth of Mattel's marketing maxim—"The doll sells the fashions and the fashions sell the doll"—is exemplified by the success of Barbie. A complete list of her outfits would fill a sizable book. Early favorites include Roman Holiday Separates, the Plantation Belle outfit (now a collector's treasure), Open Road, Busy Gal (Barbie was a fashion designer for this set, complete with a black portfolio that contained real sketches), Drum Majorette, and, of course, Wedding Day, always popular with girls of all ages.

Barbie's looks have changed over the years. That is not to say she has aged. The current Barbie looks younger than she did when she was first created. Yet, despite the makeovers, Barbie exhibits a certain anonymity, a lack of personality. That's exactly what Mattel had in mind from the beginning. The little girl who owns her will supply the personality.

"I know one of the key reasons for Barbie's success for over three decades is the open-ended nature of the doll. Barbie can

Bob Mackie's Barbie from 1990 wore the first of a series of fashions designed exclusively for Barbie by Mackie. When she was introduced, this glamorous Barbie sold for $190.

truly be anything a little girl wants to be," Ruth Handler has stated. "I envision that the possibilities for Barbie are limitless. She is only constrained by a little girl's dreams."

Through the years, in addition to undergoing makeovers to reflect the current fashions in makeup and hairstyles, Barbie has had outfits that make her a nurse, a member of every branch of the armed forces, a rock star, even an astronaut. She must have the longest and most impressive resume in the doll industry. In her first year, she was a Teen Age Fashion Model. In 1965, she was not only an Astronaut, she was also a Fashion Editor and a Student Teacher. In 1992, Barbie was a Marine Corps Sergeant, a Rap Musician, a Rollerblade In-line Skater, a Teacher, a Chef, a Businesswoman, and a Doctor. To find out what Barbie is up to this year, ask a nine-, ten-, or eleven-year old.

Barbie is also international when she's decked out in clothes derived from traditional costumes of a veritable United Nations of countries. Remember Swedish Barbie? She had Superstar Barbie's face, blond hair, and a country dress with a white lace-trimmed apron and matching bonnet. The Japanese Barbie of 1985, a truly striking doll, sold out very quickly. Brazilian Barbie looked like a participant in Carnival.

As far as dolls go, Barbie has been a model of ethnicity. She's been an African American since 1979. Some of Barbie's friends also came in black versions. Do you recall Free-Moving Brad and Free-Moving Cara? Basically, they were a black Ken and a black Barbie.

Mattel has also arranged with many corporations for special-edition Barbies; and within recent years she has become a collector's item.

Barbie has attracted the attentions and talents of top fashion

Collector's Note

The older Barbies vary in price according to condition, age, and desirability. For a couple of dollars or less, they turn up at yard sales in played-with condition. Mint-in-box Barbies can cost between $200 and $300, and rare or especially popular dolls, such as the first Barbie from 1959, can bring up to $3,500. Designer-costumed Barbies from recent years, such as Bob Mackie's 1992 Neptune Fantasy, left, can cost as much as $900.

designers and such artists as Andy Warhol, William Wegman, and Robert A.M. Stern. She inhabits toy stores, museums, and art galleries. Barbie's name and versions of her ever-changing face appear on all kinds of merchandise, including computer software, bed linens, and ice pops.

And on top of it all, Barbie is still a doll—just a doll—that is bought at a rate of about two every second.

Ken began his often rocky career as Barbie's boyfriend in 1961.

Ken

POOR KEN. FROM THE MOMENT in 1961 when he first appeared on store shelves next to Barbie, Ken has been regarded merely as another of her accessories. He has been the target of countless jokes, and, for the most part, he has been dismissed as just a sidekick in the sundry studies and celebrations of his world-famous girlfriend.

"Ken, He's a Doll," announced Mattel. That probably scared away a potentially large market of boys who had to wait until the creation of G.I. Joe, in 1964, for a figure with which they could play without being ridiculed.

The first Ken, named after the son of Ruth and Elliot Handler, was twelve inches tall. He had a crew cut with blond or brown flocked hair. His painted eyes looked straight ahead. His mouth was closed. All in all, he looked like a sensible seventeen- to-nineteen-year-old, the kind who would be pictured on the covers of those hot-rod novels, working on a roadster.

Ken came dressed in red swimming trunks, a red-and-white-striped beach jacket, and sandals. From the beginning, Ken, like his girlfriend, did a little bit of everything. Over the years, Ken has been an airline pilot, an astronaut, a bureaucratic functionary, a soldier, a sailor, a doctor, a soda jerk, and a rock star. He played the Prince in the Barbie and Ken Little Theatre, and he was a hunter with a Goin' Hunting outfit in 1964.

Ken's first-year buyers criticized his flocked hair (which tended to rub or wash off), so in the second year Ken had a molded crew cut. His face was also slimmer and his eyes were lighter in color. The next year, he shrunk half an inch, but was back up to twelve inches the following year.

It seems Ken changed in some way almost every year. His face was altered to fit the fashions of the day, his skin lightened or tanned, his hairstyle changed almost as often as Barbie's, and in recent years his body has become more muscular, more defined.

In 1969, he had bendable legs. That year, Spanish Talking Ken came out. The next year, he was Spanish Speaking Ken. Sometime in the late 1970s and early 1980s, Ken became the New Look Ken with rooted brown hair. Live Action Ken, with a jointed trunk section, joined the lineup in 1971. The next year, Ken kept pace with Barbie as Walk Lively Ken. In 1986, a realistic black Ken, named Tropical Black Ken, was introduced. That year Rocker Ken took the stage. The kinds of Kens are almost countless, although collectors do count them and keep track of them.

Regardless of how he was packaged, Ken is still Ken and he's still on the toy shelves in the stores. His claim to fame might not be his proximity to Barbie after all; it just might be a guileless knack for adapting, an inner constancy, and the ability to persevere despite some rather silly outfits and occupations. Perhaps Ken is not so poor after all.

Skipper

SKIPPER, BARBIE'S LITTLE SISTER, never was as cosmopolitan, as glamorous, or as chic as her famous sister.

Skipper was born, as dolls are, an eleven- or twelve-year-old. She was nine and a half inches tall, a slender slip of a girl with none of the curves that distinguish Barbie.

During that first year of 1964, Skipper had blond, brunette, or red hair that draped to the small of her small back. Bangs framed her face. Like her sister, Skipper had eyes that glanced to her right, but that's where the family

Skipper, added to the Barbie family in 1964, was a great companion for younger girls for whom Barbie was too sophisticated.

resemblance ended. Skipper had full cheeks. Her eyes were wide, her nose pug, her lips full. Skipper looked wholesome.

Since Skipper was Barbie's sister, naturally she had enough outfits to dress an entire small town. Skipper not only had such specially designed outfits as Silk 'n Fancy, School Girl, and Skating Fun, but she also had clothes that coordinated with Barbie's wardrobe. When your Barbie wore her Red Flair, for example, Skipper could wear her Dress Coat, which was basically a smaller version of Barbie's ensemble.

Skipper has gone through a number of changes. In 1967 she had bendable legs. A few years later, as Twist 'n Turn Skipper, she was able to dance (with the help of your hand). In the early 1970s she was Pose 'n Play Skipper and Quick Curl Skipper. In 1975 she was Growing Up Skipper, an inch and a half taller, with the hint of a bosom. Super Teen Skipper came next, as the decade turned. This Skipper was slimmer than previous versions. She was marketed as both a budding fashion model and an all-around girl who could skate or skateboard during the day and then change into an evening gown for a prom that evening.

Scooter was the first of many friends created for Barbie's sister Skipper. Scooter and Skipper could exchange outfits.

All during those busy years, Skipper acquired a number of friends. Scooter was the first. She had pigtails and freckles, and she and Skipper could exchange outfits. Ricky was one of Skipper's boyfriends. He had red hair and freckles and the same body as Skipper. In the 1970s there were also Fluff and Pose 'n Play Tiff. Growing Up Skipper chummed around with Ginger. Scott showed up in 1980. He wore a tank top, shorts, sweat jacket, and was crowned with a perm. He didn't last long. Indeed, Skipper's friends, like her outfits, came and went.

But Skipper endures. That she is still around to write about, that she flourishes in the shadow of her big sister, is not a small accomplishment. Today, Skipper looks much different from her original self. She is taller, tanner, and has large eyes.

Midge

WHILE BARBIE WAS QUICKLY BECOMING the most successful doll ever, the Handlers and the staff at Mattel began to receive letters from girls and mothers asking for a friend for Barbie. In response, in 1963 they introduced Midge.

The same size and body as Barbie, Midge was made to wear the innumerable outfits Barbie was already accumulating. Midge's blond, brunette, or red hair was shoulder length and curled up, framing her face. She had big bright painted eyes and freckles. A few of the early Midges had a line of white for a toothy smile, but most of them have a contented little closed smile. That same year, to pair with Fashion Queen Barbie, there was a Midge with molded auburn hair who came with wigs in three colors. In 1965 Midge had a new bouncy bouffant hairdo and she could bend her legs.

Two years later, Midge disappeared from the stores. Although she was named as Barbie's best friend in the marketing mythology, Midge was gone. Was there a falling out? Was she too much competition for Barbie? Did she borrow one too many outfits from Barbie and not return them?

Whatever the reason, Midge didn't return until 1987. There she was, twenty years later. She was California Midge, with more red hair, greenish eyes, and a wardrobe that was a world away from 1965. The next year she was Cool Times Midge, with even more hair. Midge was back in the swing of things. Each year she had a slightly new look. In 1991, she was a bride. With marriage came a rack of clothes specially made for her. Midge no longer had to wear castoffs from Barbie's closet.

When girls across the nation began to clamor for a friend for Barbie, Mattel introduced Midge, Barbie's best friend, in 1963. She was the same size as Barbie, so the two dolls could share Barbie's extensive wardrobe.

Although collecting Barbies has become a mania, the dolls, for the most part, were made to be played with. These five were carefully dressed by their young owner.

Although collecting Barbies has become a mania, the dolls, for the most part, were made to be played with. These five were carefully dressed by their young owner.

Barbie's Friends and Family

MATTEL DECIDED TO CREATE A FRIEND FOR KEN. So, in 1964, they introduced Allan. A television commercial announced: "Barbie and Midge are giving a surprise party in their new Dream House! The guest of honor is Mattel's new teenage doll, Allan!" Allan was slated to be Midge's boyfriend. Double-dating was a major marketing plan for the dolls. That was the year Skipper became a member of Barbie's family. She had a friend named Scooter.

Three years later, Cousin Francie appeared. According to the promotional mythology developed by Mattel, Francie was fifteen years old and mod. She wore miniskirts, maxicoats, and very "now" accessories. Of course, Francie had to have a friend. Her name was Casey. She was described as a "rebel."

Christie was Barbie's black friend. Stacy was Barbie's friend who lived in England. Walking Jamie was Barbie's pal available only through Sears, Roebuck & Company. Then there were Tutti and Todd, Barbie and Skipper's twin siblings. And they shared a friend named Chris.

In addition to her many close friends, Barbie had a number of licensed celebrity friends, including Twiggy, Julia (the television character portrayed by Diahann Carroll; the doll "talked" in a voice recorded by Carroll), Donny, Marie, and Jimmy Osmond, and Buffy and Mrs. Beasley.

Not to dismiss friendship, but the main reason for all these friends and relatives was to sell clothes. Midge could wear Barbie's clothes. Allan could wear Ken's. Skipper shared Scooter's. The more dolls you had, the more outfits you had to have. It was a simple marketing scheme. It made Mattel the nation's largest toy manufacturer, and it has made an untold number of young girls happy.

Tiny Tears

TINY TEARS WAS A CRYBABY. That's why little girls loved her. In 1950 the American Character Doll Company introduced Tiny Tears, a rubber doll with a hard-plastic head and molded hair. Five years later, she was vinyl with a hard-plastic head into which a wig of curls was rooted. This new Tiny Tears looked as much like a real baby as baby dolls did back then: she had a round face, blue eyes with thick lashes, a pinched button nose, and a tiny mouth that was open for the accompanying bottle and pacifier.

She came in a variety of sizes and had a suitable variety of names, from the hefty nineteen-inch Tiny Tears to the smallest Teeny Tiny Tears.

Each doll came with instructions for the production of tears: "Feed her only plain water. Lay her on her back and gently place the nipple in her mouth. After she has had her bottle, place the pacifier in her mouth securely and hold her in an upright position. Squeeze her body slowly and gently with both hands and she will cry REAL TEARS."

If you had Tiny Tears you certainly remember that she also had a tiny bubble pipe. You scooped up some soapy water with the bowl of the pipe, then stuck the stem into Tiny Tears' mouth. After performing a kind of Heimlich maneuver on her, she would, according to the sales literature, blow "nice big bubbles."

American Character's advertising proclaimed Tiny Tears to be "America's Best-Loved Baby Doll." Many women, who as little girls dried her tears, will certainly agree. She surely is one of the most fondly remembered dolls.

In addition to drinking, wetting, and blowing bubbles, Tiny Tears could cry, which may explain her great popularity.

Patti Playpal

IT MUST HAVE BEEN A STRANGE SIGHT on the pediatric ward. There he was, on a summer day in 1958, a man who was not a doctor, measuring children, making notes, and looking closely at all the kids.

The man was Abraham Katz, vice president of Ideal. Responsible for doll design at the company, Katz took a direct, common-sense approach to research. If you want to produce a doll that is about the same size as the child who will play with it—a doll that will be the child's companion and playmate—then you go where young children are, take out a tape measure, and size them up. Katz returned to Ideal with his findings and the next year the company introduced Patti Play Pal (as her name was spelled in 1959).

Patti was thirty-five inches tall and looked more or less like a three-year-old. She was made of blown molded vinyl. This process of construction made the doll light enough for a child to lift and to carry upstairs, downstairs, to a friend's house, and on trips.

Patti had an open, affable, pretty face. She was sculpted by Neil Estern, who was known mainly for his statues of historical figures. In this doll's face Estern tried to capture, in clay, the "incredible quality that childhood had." Realism was paramount. He didn't want to create a cartoon or a caricature of a child. Estern's wife, Anne, a designer of theatrical costumes, designed the doll's outfits and the styling of her hair. Patti had blond, auburn, brunette, black, or carrot-top orange hair that was long enough to be pulled back, with straight or curly bangs.

Your Patti Playpal, which you either selected at a store or received as a present because you were very, very good, probably wore a blue dress with appliquéd flowers or, perhaps, a red-and-white-checked dress decorated with flowers. There were other color combi-

One of Patti's greatest attractions was that she fit into a little girl's clothes. She could be dressed as your twin until you were bigger than she was.

Patti
Playpal
3 years old

Collector's Note

A Patti Playpal in
excellent condition—
a doll that wasn't a
child's play pal—sells
for up to $300 at
shows and auctions.
Peter, less popular
during his time on the
market, fetches
slightly more.

nations, but all Patti's outfits came with white bobby socks and black "patent leather" shoes. Patti Playpal was also just the size to wear your cast-off clothes, one of her main selling points. You could even dress as twins if your mother was so inclined. That first year the doll cost thirty dollars.

Patti Playpal was a big success, so big that Ideal and Estern provided an entire family for her. Peter, thirty-eight inches tall, was Patti's brother. Penny was their little sister, thirty-two inches tall, about the size of an average two-year-old. Suzy was twenty-eight inches tall, about the size of a one-year-old. Two babies, Johnny and Bonnie Playpal, both about the size of three-month-old infants, rounded out the family.

The blow-molding construction made Patti extremely practical. She was easy to wield, so a child could really play with her. The molding process, which involves melted polyethylene pellets blown into the mold, created quite a stir when Patti and her siblings made their debut. Indeed, it was the subject of international attention. A Soviet Union delegation, headed by Soviet Deputy Premier Frol Kozlov and escorted by functionaries of the U.S. State Department, visited the Ideal factory to get a close look at the blow-molding technology. In its television spots Ideal used a picture of Kozlov holding a Patti Playpal.

The day of Patti Playpal came to a close in 1962. Perhaps she was another victim of Barbie. Or maybe it was just that her time had passed. Using the 1959 mold, Ideal reissued the doll in 1981. She didn't sell. Then Ideal was sold and Patti Playpal was redesigned and produced by another company. The new doll didn't sell either.

Patti's brother Peter was three inches taller than Patti and just as adorable. He could walk with a bit of help.

Trolls

TROLLS ARE SO UGLY, THEY ARE CUTE. They look like a mixture of frog, monkey, and nightmare. Their hair is psychedelic and stands on end. Their eyes are big and eager. And they are always smiling. Only another troll—or a child—could love a troll.

The recent resurgence of trolls elicits a sense of déjà vu in parents who, thirty or so years ago, begged and scrimped to populate their rooms with the creatures.

Inspired by the mischievous characters of Scandinavian folklore, troll dolls were first made in 1952 by Helena and Martii Kuuskoskif of Finland. At first, they just made them as toys for their children. That turned into a business and eventually they sold about one hundred and fifty thousand of their trolls, which they called Fauni Trolls.

The trolls' invasion of America began in the late 1950s when Thomas Dam, a Danish woodcarver, made his version of a troll for his daughter. She showed it to her friends. By the early 1960s, Dam had three factories turning out "Dammit" dolls or "Dam Things." By 1963, college coeds—the barome-

ter of trends—were packing trolls along with their books. It was reported that the trolls brought good luck.

Shortly afterward, trolls were everywhere. According to those who keep count, trolls were the second most popular doll during the 1960s. Barbie, of course, was number one.

At first, trolls, like people, were naked. Then, like Barbie, they were transformed by clothing into soldiers, clowns, superheroes, astronauts, even Santa.

Trolls hung from rearview mirrors; they were on stationery, pencils, T-shirts, soap; they were made into jewelry; they were banks, lawn ornaments, lamps, cookie cutters, and candy. Trolls, decked out in bridal gowns and tuxedos, were given as wedding gifts. There were trolls called Grooves. These brandished such messages as "Tell it like it is!" and "Outasight!"

The popularity of trolls seemed to fade during the 1970s. In the late 1980s, however, trolls were sighted again. Norfins, trolls by a new name but made by the same company that made the Dam trolls in the 1960s, proliferated. Trolls are definitely back—and they are as adorably ugly as ever.

Trolls have been with us for many years. They come in a variety of shapes and sizes, but they have one thing in common—they are all adorably ugly.

1960–1968

THE 1960S WAS AN AGE OF YOUTH AND IDEALISM, and a time of social and political turmoil. The youth culture was reflected in the strident voice of those who welcomed the Beatles, protested the Vietnam War, and attended Woodstock. Forty-three-year-old John F. Kennedy was elected President of the United States, the youngest man to hold that office.

The 1960s brought nuclear power, from nuclear-powered spacecraft and submarines to power plants that produced cheap electricity. In 1962, John Glenn Jr. became the first American astronaut to circle the earth. Russian Yuri Gagarin had been the first man in space, followed by the first American, Alan Shephard Jr. By the end of the decade Neil Armstrong had made his "giant leap for mankind" on the moon.

The civil rights movement, which had begun in the 1950s in the South, spread. Black influence grew in some areas, especially in sports, and in music with the arrival of the popular Motown sound. But the struggle for integration was difficult, and such terms as "sit-ins" and "freedom riders" became part of the American vocabulary. Finally the Civil Rights Act was passed.

The involvement of the United States in the Vietnam War was a controversial issue that ignited protests on college campuses across the country. A counterculture developed among the young. Some, looking for a more beautiful world, escaped the real one by submerging themselves in mysticism or the

drug culture. These peace-loving young men and women, called "hippies" or "flower children," influenced the look of the times. Art and fabrics were bright with vivid "Day-Glo" hues. At Woodstock, a town in upstate New York, young people converged for a festival: three days of peace and music. *Hair* was the first rock musical, "the age of Aquarius" cry for a time of peace and understanding.

Fashions became "less" with the introduction of the miniskirt and a topless bathing suit for women. Along with the Beatles' shaggy haircuts came fashions from the British Isles. Mary Quent and Twiggy influenced the way women dressed in the later years of the decade as much as Jacqueline Kennedy had influenced them in the early years.

Women also became more militant. The National Organization for Women was formed. Birth control pills became available for the first time, giving women a new sexual freedom.

The dolls of the '60s reflected a wide range of concerns and interests. The teen fashion model, Barbie, became even more popular. She was given a boyfriend, a sister, and friends, as well as a car and other symbols of affluence. A male counterpart was developed by Hasbro. Called G.I. Joe, he was not just a doll intended to appeal to boys—he was an "action figure." He also had costumes, mostly military uniforms, and such accessories as weapons, jeeps, and tanks. His popularity waned, however, as negative feelings about Vietnam intensified.

Chatty Cathy

LITTLE GIRLS HAVE ALWAYS TALKED TO THEIR DOLLS—but Chatty Cathy was the first to talk back. Created by Mattel, she made her debut at the 1960 International Toy Fair in New York City. Freckled, bright-eyed, and cute, with two teeth protruding from her slight smile, Chatty Cathy knew eleven phrases.

The first Chatty Cathy was twenty-one inches tall and looked like a five-year-old. She had blond hair and wore either a two-piece red playsuit or a blue party dress. Her all-important voice box was buried in her chest.

Chatty Cathy's looks changed a little each year. In her second year she became a brunette with new vinyl limbs and a redesigned speaker. In 1963 Chatty Cathy had auburn hair and seven more phrases. She said things like: "Do you love me?" "Give me a kiss." "Please brush my hair." "I'm so tired." "Let's have a party." "Let's play school."

This talkative little girl was so popular that immediately a variety of accessories appeared in toy stores. There was a wardrobe, a stroller, a cradle, a bed, a tea cart, and the "9-Way Stroll-A-Buggy." And, of course, there was a large selection of clothes as well as patterns for clothes.

Chatty Cathy could wear the Nursery School outfit (a yellow A-line dress trimmed in red and blue) or the Playtime ensemble (denim shorts, white T-shirt, red-and-white striped jacket, and sun visor). Sunny Day consisted of six pieces—red, blue, and green capri pants, a top, a cap, and sandals. After a full day she could be dressed for Sleepytime in rosebud print flannel pajamas and a matching sleep cap.

As a result of Cathy's popularity, a family of related dolls was created. Chatty Baby and Tiny Chatty Baby appeared in 1962. Chatty Baby was eighteen inches tall and like her little sister, who was fifteen inches small, could say eleven phrases. The next year there was Chatty's cousin, Charmin' Chatty.

Singin' Chatty, a doll who could sing her own renditions of "Row, Row, Row Your Boat" and "Ring Around the Roses," took the stage in 1965. By that time Cathy Chatty had run out of things to say, and she faded from the scene. Mattel tried to revive her in 1970, but she didn't look the same and didn't sell well.

Chatty Cathy, who looked like a bright, cute five-year-old, was the first doll who could talk—and she was an immediate success.

Charmin' Chatty

CHARMIN' CHATTY CONTINUED THE CONVERSATION Chatty Cathy started. This doll, produced by Mattel in the early 1960s, was a loquacious companion. She could speak on a number of subjects and play board games with you.

Chatty was made of plastic and vinyl. Her hair (either auburn or platinum blond) was rooted and hung straight with bangs. She had sleep eyes that were directed humorously to the side and her mouth was closed in an endearing, dimple-cheeked smile.

Charmin' Chatty came in a red, white, and blue sailor suit with red tights and white-and-blue shoes. She also wore black plastic wire-rimmed glasses. (Usually, after a couple of days at home, she went without her glasses. They had been lost or her eyesight had improved dramatically.)

Charmin' Chatty was one of the most appealing dolls of the 1960s. She looked friendly. You just knew she was good company. Her voice came from three-inch white plastic records that you inserted in a slot in her side, just under her left arm. Pull the string in her back and she chatted. A speaker was located in her chest.

There was a record with every costume set and her conversation was appropriate for each outfit. The Pajama Party set, for example, included a pink and white rosebud print cotton nightgown, pink slippers, curlers, and a hair net. On one side of the record she chatted about restaurants and shopping and made animal noises. On the other she recited Proverbs and Poems to Get Acquainted. Charmin' Chatty's most expensive play set included a coat and hat for travel, a foreign language dictionary (small enough for her to use), and a record that enabled her to speak in several languages and translate her words into English. This set cost about eight dollars, not an insubstantial sum at the time.

The board games you could play with Charmin' Chatty were Chatty Skate 'N Slide, Chatty at the Fair, Chatty Animal Round Up, and Chatty Animal Friend. The games were sold two to a box and each game came with a record of responses.

Charmin' Chatty was definitely a winner.

A most appealing doll, Charmin' Chatty looked like she had a sense of humor. In addition to talking, she could play board games.

Miss Ideal

MISS IDEAL WAS "THE PHOTOGRAPHER'S MODEL." Made by the company she was named after, Miss Ideal's year in the spotlight, and on store shelves, was 1961. She came in a blue-green and pink box, decorated with stylized cartoons of photographers' spotlights and faces of women, and a silhouette of a classic model's pose.

Miss Ideal was a big doll—twenty-five or thirty inches. She was all vinyl and had nylon rooted blond, brunette, or, rarely, platinum hair. She came with a beauty kit that contained a comb, curlers, and wave lotion. You could "set her nylon hair, like a real permanent." Her original price was sixteen dollars for the twenty-five-inch model and twenty dollars for the thirty-inch doll.

Miss Ideal had a pleasant face with big sleep eyes, a cute nose, and a nice smile. She looked like a small version of Daddy's Girl, an Ideal companion doll that appeared about the same time. Side by side, except for the difference in size, the dolls looked like twins, although Miss Ideal had a wider, chubbier face and looked younger than Daddy's Girl. Both dolls were sculpted by Neil Estern, who was also responsible for the Patti Playpal dolls.

She was flexible and posable, as a "photographer's model" should be. With jointed ankles, wrists, arms, legs, and waist she could "twist and turn" as if she were at a fashion shoot. Her wardrobe, however, was not what one would expect to see in high-fashion magazine layouts. Your Miss Ideal might have worn Town and Country, which was a simple green (or blue) sundress with a pinafore and a bandanna. Perhaps on another day she wore a checked dress, campus jacket, and a straw hat. Nothing elaborate, nothing glamorous.

Miss Ideal had only one year. In 1962 she became Terry Twist. Remember her? She was dressed in a cheerleader's outfit, a white *I* (for Ideal) on her red shirt. And she had a megaphone on which her name was stenciled.

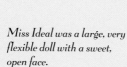

Miss Ideal was a large, very flexible doll with a sweet, open face.

Tammy

TAMMY MOVED INTO THE NEIGHBORHOOD IN 1962. She was Ideal's answer to Mattel's Barbie. Tammy wore less makeup and was more wholesome looking. She was pretty, not beautiful; she resembled the girl who lived next door. According to the little booklet that came with Tammy, she was "the doll you love to dress."

The basic Tammy was twelve inches tall and was dressed in a blue-and-white cotton jumpsuit and sneakers. Like other teenage fashion dolls, Tammy was the sum and variety of her outfits.

How many of Tammy's outfits can you remember? One of the favorites was School Daze—a very 1960s wool plaid and corduroy school dress, pinched in with a wide gold belt at Tammy's incredibly narrow waist. Along with the dress came a tiny typewriter (manual, of course), the essential telephone, and a portfolio with a zipper. Another popular outfit was Walking Her Pet, which consisted of a skirt and plaid top, a locket, a red shoulder bag, matching scarf, and, naturally, a dog on a leash. And let's not forget Fun in the Sun, Beau and Arrow, Cutie Co-ed, Ring-A-Ding, Sorority Sweetheart, and Snowbunny.

After a day of walking the pooch, going to school, and playing in the sun or the snow, Tammy could be dressed in her Sleepytime outfit, which came with baby-doll pajamas, curlers, a comb, slippers, and a lilliputian glass of milk to ensure sweet dreams.

In 1964 Tammy acquired a family—Dad and Mom, brothers Ted and Pete, and sister Pepper. Each had a large wardrobe. The next year Tammy had a boyfriend named Bud.

Attempting to keep up with Barbie, Tammy was, for a while anyway, a marketing star—with books, records, and a board game. But she disappeared after 1964. There was just no stopping Barbie.

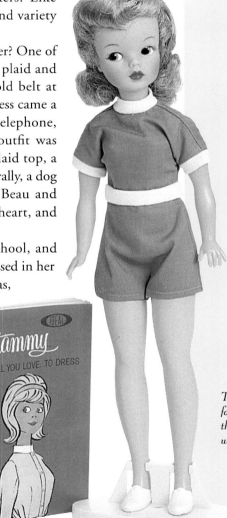

Tammy was the teenage fashion doll who looked like the girl next door— wholesome and pretty.

Tressy

Tressy was the first doll whose hair grew and could be styled in a number of different ways.

TRESSY WAS ONE OF MANY TEENAGE FASHION DOLLS produced, if not to compete with Barbie, then to cut in on Barbie's success. By 1963, when Tressy appeared, that success was resulting in the manufacture of more than six million Barbies a year. Tressy, made by American Character Doll Company, might have been merely another vinyl fashion plate, except for one thing—her hair "grew."

Even if you only vaguely remember Tressy or any of her period outfits, you remember how her hair worked. You pulled a strand (called the "secret strand" in promotional literature) at the top of her head. The hair unwound, doing its Rapunzel thing. A little girl could spend an afternoon styling it into hairdos with such names as Beehive Bubble, Royal Pouf, and Beach Beauty Bob. A booklet with instructions for six "Easy-To-Make Hair Styles for Hi-fashion Tressy HER HAIR GROWS!" accompanied each doll. A larger booklet of instruction—a hairdo how-to manual—was published in 1965 by Dell. It was titled *Tressy's Hair Glamour—Her Own Magazine of Hair Care.*

Tressy's looks were competitive with Barbie's. Her vinyl skin had a creamy tone and her face seemed friendlier than Barbie's. She also felt substantial for a doll that cost just under five dollars.

Tressy was joined almost immediately by a little sister, Cricket, whose hair also grew, and a friend, Mary Make-Up. Although Tressy, Cricket, and Mary Make-Up did not have the wardrobe of Barbie and her friends, they did have more than enough outfits.

Tressy's last year was 1965. She wasn't around long enough to acquire a boyfriend. She simply faded into the 1960s. Now, more than thirty years later, you might not remember her name or her face, but you'll never forget that hair! You pulled it out and you brushed it and braided it and then untangled it. Then, when you were finished, you took a little key, fit it into a hole in her back—and just wound it back in.

Crissy

CRISSY, IDEAL TOY CORPORATION'S MOD TEENAGE fashion doll, moved into stores in 1968. Girls loved her so much that the toy company followed Crissy with an entire family.

Made of hard plastic and vinyl, Crissy had a gimmick that enabled her to lure a few sales away from Barbie—this was her retractable red hair. Do you remember how it was done? You pushed Crissy's belly button to release the hair, then you pulled on her red tresses. For a short look, you wound the small, flesh-colored knob in her back to draw the hair back into her head. Retractable hair was evidently a family trait; every doll in the family—Velvet, Cinnamon, Kerry (Crissy's Irish cousin), Mia, Brandi, and all the others—had "growing hair."

Crissy usually had her hair braided into a long ponytail when she came from the store. But it could be brushed, curled, and pinned up in any number of styles.

When Crissy first appeared, she wore an orange miniskirt, a long-sleeved top, and orange plastic Mary Jane shoes. A black Crissy was introduced in 1970. This was basically the same doll with soft dark skin. The same year, Look Around Crissy showed up on the toy shelves; when you pulled a string in her neck, her head turned from side to side.

The next year, a black Moovin' Groovin' Crissy and a white Moovin' Groovin' edition made the scene. Both dolls wore orange outfits. And so it went. Every year there were new members of Crissy's family and new outfits to satisfy the most fashion-conscious girl.

Today, Crissy satisfies collectors who want to hold on to a bit of their own moovin' groovin' girlhoods.

Baby Crissy's hair grew, too. Made by Ideal, she didn't appear until 1972.

Crissy was another popular doll whose hair grew. Here she is with her hair at various lengths.

123

Littlechap Family

DURING THE 1960S, REMCO INDUSTRIES made the Littlechap Family. The dolls were a marketer's vision of the ideal American family in vinyl. John, the man of the family, coincidently had the same first name as President Kennedy. His wife looked not unlike the First Lady.

"Never before," maintained the copy on the package, "has a family of dolls been created that is so true to life."

The story of the Littlechaps was printed on the back of the family's outfit packages.

"Meet the Littlechap family: Dr. John Littlechap; Lisa, his wife; their two daughters—17-year-old Judith and 10-year-old Libby." Judith—her friends called her Judy—was an honor student at Lanesville High School. She "loves parties and crazy desserts." Libby was ten years old, a fifth grader at the elementary school. She "loves to climb trees, pester her sister, and wants to be a doctor like her daddy."

Libby was ten and a half inches tall. Her rooted brown hair was pulled back in a ponytail. Her features were painted and her cheeks had deep dimples. Judy stood twelve inches tall. She had short brown hair and dimples, which seemed to run in the family.

Lisa Littlechap was the attractive mother of Judith and Libby. She was a "former model—wonderful cook—President of the P.T.A., and best-dressed woman in town." In other words, she was the perfect helpmate for "Dr. John Littlechap, member of the Lanesville County Medical Society, former flight surgeon U.S. Army Air Force, loves his family and golf, wishes he could find more time for both."

This dream family was expensive. The entire family cost one hundred and thirty-five dollars. And then there were the outfits and accessories. Cardboard play sets—stages on which the Littlechaps stiffly played—were available. These included the doctor's office, the Littlechaps' family room, the girls' room, complete with pictures of movie stars, school pennants, and a portable record player, and John and Lisa's master bedroom.

Each room was portable. The furniture could be neatly stored inside and a plastic handle was attached to the top. A snap at the end of the handle held the room closed and compact while you carried it to a friend's house.

Remco did not skimp on the details. The doctor's black plastic medical bag contained a plastic thermometer, a medicine bottle, reflex hammer, tongue depressor, stethoscope, and even a tiny hypodermic syringe. And how could anyone keep track of all the lilliputian accessories that could be scattered about Dr. Littlechap's office, including eyeglasses, miniature medical books, a ballpoint pen, pipe, tobacco pouch, and a patient's chart on a tiny clipboard?

The Littlechaps didn't last long. John Kennedy's assassination made them a ghoulish relic and they were discontinued.

Marketed as the perfect American family, the four Littlechaps had many outfits and accessories, including cardboard play sets.

Poor Pitiful Pearl

*Patterned after William
Steig's delightful little
character, Poor Pitiful Pearl
was irresistible.*

POOR PITIFUL PEARL, A CHARACTER CREATED BY the writer and cartoonist William Steig, became a doll in 1957. Manufactured by the Brookglad Corporation, she was eighteen inches tall and was made of soft vinyl. She could sit, stand, bend, and kneel. She had long, rooted saran hair. And according to the copy that accompanied the doll, her purpose—besides play—was to teach good grooming habits.

Pearl's face makes her memorable. It was an engaging, even adorable, cartoon face with a nub of a nose, poochy cheeks, and a simple (yet contented) line of a smile. Her ears looked like tiny handles on the sides of a jug. She wore a plain, ragged polka-dot or floral print dress and a simple matching kerchief.

Pearl was two inches shorter her second year out. Fortunately, the face was the same. She "pulls at the heartstrings . . . opens the purse strings of America's Doll Market," claimed an advertisement that ran in *Playthings* magazine. "Pearl needs TLC (Tender Loving Care) . . ." the ad continued.

Horsman took over production of Pearl during the early 1960s. This Pearl, who had shorter hair, was also sixteen inches tall, and was dressed in the same ragged dress, dotted with flower blossoms, and kerchief that was a copy of the original Steig illustration.

Little Brother and Little Sister

LITTLE BROTHER AND LITTLE SISTER, imported in 1967 from France by Creative Playthings of New Jersey, were the first so-called anatomically correct play dolls to shake up the American toy market and the nation's nurseries. These adorable siblings were twenty inches tall, all vinyl, and had sleep eyes. They also had genitalia, which fanned quite a fuss. Appropriately, the dolls were banned in Boston. They continued to sell, however, and were available in stores and through some catalogs until the early 1970s.

And then there was Archie Bunker's grandson, Joey Stivic. When Gloria and Meathead, of the popular and controversial television show *All in the Family*, had a son, the Ideal Toy Corporation was prompted to produce a doll that, to use the phrase on the package, was "a physically correct male."

"A little girl will love playing mommy to a baby boy for a change . . . especially sweet Joey Stivic with blue eyes, rooted hair, soft vinyl skin, and winning smile," ran the copy on the side of the box.

Joey was released in 1976. He was about fifteen inches long, with a vinyl head and a hard-plastic body. The eyes were painted blue; the hair was blond. He was a drink-and-wet doll, so he came with a small plastic bottle, two disposable diapers, and a blue flannel blanket. Also in the box was a flyer with care instructions. Illustrations showed the play mother how to change diapers and operate the bottle. After feeding, "Hold baby in your arms as you burp him. After holding him upright for a while, he will wet his diaper . . . just like all babies do after they've been fed. And now, it is time to change his diaper."

It all seemed fairly straightforward, but the Joey Stivic doll ruffled the sensibilities of a number of conservative groups who objected to the doll. Joey Stivic was sold for only a few months before Ideal withdrew the doll from the market.

Joey Stivic, Archie Bunker's grandson, was available for only a few months because there was a public outcry about his "anatomical correctness."

Little Brother and Little Sister, the first anatomically correct dolls in the United States, were banned in Boston.

G.I. Joe

G.I. Joe, always called "an action figure," disproved the conviction of almost everyone in the toy industry that a doll for boys would not sell.

G.I. JOE WAS A BARBIE FOR BOYS. That's how Stanley Weston conceived him. Weston, an independent toy designer, pitched the idea of a jointed, articulated soldier figure to Don Levine of Hasbro. Weston wanted to base the figure on the hero of a television series, *The Lieutenant,* scheduled to air that fall.

Levine liked the idea. But the television series turned out to be a soap opera aimed at adults. (The producer of the program, Gene Rodenberry, took his "soap opera" to outer space and called it *Star Trek.*) The toy tie-in was canceled. Still, the concept of a military doll stayed with Levine. Then, on a cold day in February 1963, Levine, while walking in New York City, spotted a sculptor's jointed wooden mannequin in the display window of an arts supply store.

That was it! A soldier the size of a Barbie doll, but very movable. (All Barbie could do at the time was pose stiffly or recline by a pool.) This doll, Levine thought, would have to engage in combat. Levine pitched the concept all the way up to the president. Hasbro bought it. It has been reported that Weston, the man with the original idea, received a lump sum of one hundred thousand dollars and relinquished any claim to royalties.

At first, Levine had encountered resistance to the project. "A boy will never play with a doll" was a constant refrain. Consequently, this new toy was developed and referred to as a "movable soldier," or an "action figure."

As production progressed, Levine added a scar to the soldier's right cheek. This imbued the doll with a toughness, and it was also an identifying feature that provided some protection against patent infringement. The figure was eleven and a half inches tall, because Barbie was that height. The body was made of sturdy styrene plastic. Ball and socket joints, rivets, and connector studs gave it flexibility. The twenty-one movable parts were held together with elastic bands and metal hooks.

The figure had everything except a name, and Hasbro's advertising agency pressured Levine for one name to cover the range of dolls. Levine had no ideas, until one night when he watched an old movie on television. The movie was *The Story of G.I. Joe.* The name fit neatly into place. G.I., which stands for Government Issue, was short and strong, and, thanks to the movie and to the many fathers who might be induced to buy G.I. Joe for their sons, it was readily recognizable.

They now had the doll—or, rather, the movable action figure—and the name. All that was required were the things that sell dolls—accessories. Hasbro's design team consulted U.S. Army training manuals and made every effort to reproduce accurately, in miniature, everything from battle fatigues to dress uniforms to a vast array of weapons for each of the branches of the armed forces.

G.I. Joe's first victory was the defeat of the toy industry's prejudice against boy dolls or a doll for boys. G.I. Joe was sold as America's Movable Fighting Man. And it wasn't long after Hasbro's flashy debut (complete with a film for the toy firm's representatives, portraying G.I. Joe as a fighting man) that G.I. Joe was laying siege to toy stores across the country.

G.I. Joe cost about four dollars. The various uniform and equipment sets ran from one dollar to about five. As with Barbie, much of G.I. Joe's success can be attributed to all the extra stuff. By the end of the first year, there were six uniforms and sixty-three equipment sets for the "Action" sailor, pilot, soldier, and Marine. The toy shelves looked like an Army-Navy surplus store. And that first year more than two million G.I. Joes were sold.

To cap off 1964, Hasbro set up the Official G.I. Joe Club. One hundred and fifty thousand kids signed up almost immediately. A membership cost only fifty cents. Here's what you received: a complete catalog of G.I. Joe equipment ("One of the most fascinating catalogs ever printed," according to advertisements), an identification card for your wallet, a membership certificate to frame and hang in your room, an iron-on transfer for your T-shirt, and a "special regulation Dog Tag stamped with your name and your official G.I. Joe membership number."

The second year G.I. Joe's sales doubled. A black G.I. Joe was introduced, initially only in northern cities. In addition,

Collector's Note

A played-with G.I. Joe can be bought for pocket change at flea markets, but collectors pay $50 to $200 for desirable figures in good condition. Some G.I. Joe boxed sets can bring as much as $1,000.

there was now a Combat Jeep Set for the fighting men. In the wagon that the jeep pulled was a battery-operated searchlight, which, the accompanying brochure stated, could be used to send Morse code. A cannon capable of firing small rockets rode in the back of the jeep. The set cost fifteen dollars. By the second year, there were eighty G.I. Joe equipment sets. There were also G.I. Joe gift sets sold only at Sears, Roebuck & Company. The G.I. Joe Machine Gun Emplacement Set, for example, included a G.I. Joe, sandbags, a .50 caliber machine gun on a tripod, an ammunition case, and ten other pieces of equipment.

Over the years, G.I. Joe has spun off board games (like "Let's Go Joe"), a fleet of vehicles (including an amphibious personnel carrier, helicopter, and police motorcycle), and equipment for kids—Backyard Patrol sets—so they could be like Joe. With these sets, a boy could strap a .45 (with holster) to his belt, don the camouflage helmet, and, packing his mess kit, canteen, and walkie-talkie set, he could while away a Sunday afternoon in combat.

The 1960s saw Talking G.I. Joe with Kung-Fu Grip and Major Mike Powers/Atomic man, an eleven-and-a-half-inch secret agent. As the decade drew to a close, Adventure packs appeared. Each pack contained between thirteen and twenty-four pieces of equipment. G.I. Joe, forever in search of new equipment and new and exciting missions, became G.I. Adventure Team in the 1970s. The adventures became wilder ("Search for the Abominable Snowman") and it seems most of the Joes sprouted backwoods beards. Super Joe (whose mission was defending the universe) landed on the shelves in 1977. Super Joe was only eight and a half inches tall (due to the oil crisis, which forced the price of plastics up), but he was a science fiction superhero and he fought such futuristic monsters as Gor, King of the Terrons, with his red "destructo ray."

This phase passed and led to G.I. Joe's career as a three-and-three-quarter-inch action figure. Spurred on by the success of the Star Wars figures, the 1982 G.I. Joe, almost twenty years old, appeared as G.I. Joe: A Real American Hero. The dolls had now become a team of good guys with names like Grunt, Snake Eyes, and Rock 'n Roll. They were pitched against the forces of COBRA. Each character had his own specialized role, weapons, and ID card on the back of the package.

G.I. Joe returned to his original size as part of Hasbro's Hall of Fame line. At first, Hasbro produced sixty thousand "dolls," but customers—both kids and parents who wanted their own children to play with what they had—lined up and orders poured in. Hasbro produced thirty thousand more, and by that Christmas, the figure had sold out.

Then production stopped, but in 1993 G.I. Joe was back. Drawn from an animated television and comic book series, the new Joes are called G.I. Joe Extreme. They are five inches tall and look as if they have consumed massive amounts of steroids. What will come after Extreme?

A vast assortment of armaments, equipment, and outfits were made for G.I. Joe.

Penny Brite

PENNY BRITE WAS CREATED AS COMPETITION for Barbie. Although she didn't knock Barbie off her pedestal, for several years this cute, perky girl next door put on a good show.

"The Wonderful World of Penny Brite," to use the title of a pamphlet that came with the doll, began in 1963. Made by Topper Toys, she was shorter than the other teenage fashion dolls that were then flooding the market. Only about eight inches tall, she seemed like a little sister, a model for younger young ladies. She was made of vinyl and was fully jointed.

Penny Brite had an adorable face. She was always smiling and had dimpled cheeks. Her head tilted toward you and her painted eyes looked to the side, as if she were about to share an amusing secret.

By her second year, she had wire armatures in her legs and arms, making her very posable. That year, she cost one dollar and twenty-nine cents and came in a plastic case with a handle. The handle pushed inside the case, becoming a clothes rack and converting the case to a wardrobe.

Fresh from the store, Penny Brite wore a red and white dress. A red bow adorned her bubble-cut hair. Although she was undeniably cute, her outfits made her a success and now make her memorable. There was Chit Chat, composed of black velvet pants, a white printed top with "Chit Chat" on it, a black hair bow, red shoes, and a red telephone book. Or how about Singing in the Rain, with advertising copy that went something like this: "Let it rain! Let it rain! Penny Brite will never complain in her black-and-white-checked raincoat trimmed with red corduroy, matching hat, matching umbrella, red boots." Remember Sun and Fun, Winter Princess, Anchors Aweigh, or Flower Girl?

The clothes were well made for doll clothes. They were completely hemmed, with pleats, buttons, applied trims, even appliqués. Coats were lined and every dress was made of cotton and made in America.

For a few more dollars, you could bring home one of Penny Brite's play sets, which were, as the copy on the packages asserted, fully assembled and ready to play. Kitchen Dinette was as

"real as life." Travel Set was for "a doll who travels in style."
Penny Brite could go to the Beauty Parlor, play in her Bedroom
Set, or go to the School Room, in which "Penny Brite learns her
ABCs like a real little girl."

Eventually, the little girls who played with Penny Brite
moved on to Barbie. By the early 1970s, Penny Brite was history.

*Only eight inches tall, Penny Brite
was a little-girl doll who had lots of
outfits and accessories.*

1970-1979

THE DECADE OF THE BICENTENNIAL of the United States brought with it an emerging awareness of environmental concerns. In 1970 the first Earth Day was observed. Soon afterward the Environmental Protection Agency was organized and private organizations like Greenpeace came into being.

The Watergate scandal stayed in the news until President Richard Nixon finally resigned. Revelations of corruption and abuse of power in the White House held television audiences mesmerized, as did a documentary about family life in which members of a California family, the Louds, were followed by cameras. The twelve hours with the Louds resulted in greater public awareness of the family stresses caused by divorce and homosexuality. The history of a fictional black family was traced in *Roots*, a television series based on Alex Haley's book.

Pure entertainment encompassed Archie Bunker's bigotry in *All in the Family*, the domestic life of mob figures in *The Godfather*, and the horror of Stephen King's *Carrie* in both movie and book form. It also included the *Star Wars* films of George Lucas, on which highly collectible toys and dolls were based.

The VCR became a reality, and television shows could be recorded at any time to be watched later. Videotape rental stores proliferated—the era of the couch potato had begun!

But communication was not cut off, and the CB radio became a craze. Not just truckers, but all "good buddies" could chat with each other on the road.

For those who preferred the night life away from television, there was disco. The movie *Saturday Night Fever* gives a taste of the glitzy dance craze. Strobe lights and fancy clothing were part of the distinctive disco style. Another kind of pop music also appeared in the '70s: punk rock. In a revolt against the establishment, punks went for shock value, like piercing cheeks with safety pins.

Science was going into science fiction areas: CAT scans, which could give cross sectional pictures of the body, and test-tube babies. Sex was openly discussed, "everything you wanted to know" was published. This fixation even entered the doll world. The National Organization for Women condemned ten companies, including the doll manufacturer Mattel, for sexist advertising.

The dolls of the '70s were a product of their times. More and more ethnic dolls were made, and anatomically correct dolls appeared on toy store shelves. Barbie still reigned supreme. Not only could she grow hair, but she also had new celebrity friends and a brother, Baby Brother Tenderlove.

Holly Hobbie

HOLLY HOBBIE was the little doll who wore the big calico sun bonnet and the country dress and became a big, big business. She was created by and named after Holly Ulinskas Hobbie, who in 1966 was encouraged by her brother-in-law to submit some of her watercolor paintings to the American Greetings Corporation of Cleveland, Ohio. Although the company generally did not accept unsolicited art, they decided to use Hobbie's paintings, illustrating homey verses, as an experimental line of greeting cards.

In a year Hobby, who had studied art at Pratt Institute in New York and painting at Boston University, had a contract and the character was on her way to fame. An advertisement for Holly Hobbie cards in a fashion magazine stirred up interest among manufacturers who wanted to use the little girl's picture on products. By the 1970s a house could be furnished with Holly Hobbie items. Her image appeared on more than three hundred products, including wallpaper, dinnerware, candles, cookies, sunglasses, and nightgowns. There were also many Holly Hobbie games and toys and, of course, a Holly Hobbie doll.

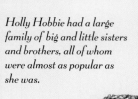

Holly Hobbie had a large family of big and little sisters and brothers, all of whom were almost as popular as she was.

The Knickerbocker Toy Company introduced the Holly Hobbie doll in 1975. The cloth doll with stitched features, wearing the trademark ruffly bonnet and dress, was immediately successful. Holly had charm, a wholesomeness and a rural freshness found only in toys and other dolls, like Raggedy Ann, created around the turn of the century. Holly didn't have dazzle. And for many girls, that was—and is—her selling point. A family of dolls, from Baby Holly to Grandma Hobbie, soon followed Holly Hobbie into the nation's stores and homes.

In 1980, just as Holly Hobbie's day of peak popularity was drawing to a close, Those Characters from Cleveland, a division of American Greetings,

Here we have Holly, Carrie (in red), Heather, and Robby.

introduced Strawberry Shortcake. This doll, thirteen inches tall, though not officially part of the Holly Hobbie family, certainly looked like a distant cousin. She, too, was made of cloth and wore a big bonnet and an apron. Her red hair and the strawberry print on her clothing reflected her name.

Then in 1989 Holly Hobbie made a comeback. American Greetings brought her back for a second generation, with Mattel Toys producing the second wave of Hollys. The new rag dolls, with only slight alterations in dress, came in a variety of sizes. Good wholesome nostalgia will always be on the cutting edge of fashion.

Barefoot Children

The Barefoot Children, created by German doll maker Annette Himstedt, signaled the appearance of modern dolls that were both toys and collectibles. Songa, right, a Timeless Creations doll, was designed by Himstedt and produced by Mattel in 1992. Adrienne (opposite page) was vinyl and was made by Mattel in 1989.

IN THE 1970S A SUBTLE CHANGE BEGAN to take place in the world of dolls. Making reproductions of antique bisque dolls became a serious hobby when molds of French and German dolls became available. Ceramic shops began to promote doll-making classes. Thousands of people bought unpainted porcelain doll heads and painted their own versions of dolls' faces that were popular fifty years earlier.

Eventually, after learning the technical side of porcelain doll making, artists, many of whom were amateurs, started to sculpt their own dolls, and even began to make their own molds and produce their own original dolls. This trend led to the creation of character faces, which were similar to the expressive and realistic dolls that were popular after 1910. The cycle was beginning again—a revolt against the familiar, cute "dolly" faces.

It was artists in the United States who started the trend, but before long creative doll making had spread to Germany and other European countries. Germany has had a long tradition of doll making, and extremely innovative German artists began to create stunning naturalistic, individualistic dolls that were on the cutting edge of doll design.

Collectors of antique dolls soon learned about these exquisite modern dolls and began to acquire them in bisque versions, which were often quite expensive. When it became obvious that there was a broad market for the new character dolls, some artists experimented with producing their dolls in vinyl. By using plastic as a medium, many dolls could be produced more economically, making them more affordable and of greater appeal to the general public.

The Barefoot Children by Annette Himstedt are among the loveliest of these dolls. A self-taught doll artist, Himstedt lives near Hamburg, Germany, and has been creating her unique dolls since 1979. Himstedt's vinyl dolls are produced in Spain and until recently were distributed on a wide scale in the United States by Timeless Creations, a division of Mattel. These large dolls are beautiful enough to appeal to adults, but sturdy enough to make durable toys for children. They have romantic names like Kasimir, Ayoka, Fiene, and Annchen. They often fill the bill as "grandmother dolls": grandmother buys one and allows her grandchildren to play with it, but also enjoys having that vinyl child to herself when the children go home.

1980–1989

THE 1980S HAS BEEN DESCRIBED as the decade of conspicuous consumption. It might also be described as the digital age, or the age of electronics. Although fax machines and computers had been around for some time, it wasn't until the 1980s that they became ubiquitous. Compact discs began to replace records and tapes. Camcorders appeared on the scene, as did video games. Even more exciting was the concept of virtual reality. Digitally simulated "cybernauts," wearing headsets and gloves, could experience and interact with an imaginary three-dimensional world.

In the real world a new disease, and later, the virus causing it, was discovered. The first case of AIDS was seen in the United States in 1981 and in a couple of years it had multiplied to thousands of cases. In the real world there was also a crack cocaine epidemic and serious concern about the number of people who were homeless. People tied yellow ribbons around trees, or anything else handy, as a way of expressing hope for fifty-two Americans who had been captured and held hostage in Iran. And they watched on television as the space shuttle *Challenger* exploded.

The 1980s was a decade of reckoning in certain areas of the American industry. Car makers were the worst hit—challenged by the influx of automobiles from Japan. Electronics manufacturers also had heavy competition from other countries. For the first time the trade balance had Americans importing products rather than exporting to the rest of the world.

The status of women reached a new height when Sandra Day O'Connor was confirmed as a Supreme Court judge and when women were accepted for training as astronauts. The National Museum of Women in the Arts, in Washington, D.C., became a reality. Women were more often seen at executive levels in business and industry.

Television was in the age of the daytime talk shows. Roseanne appeared in a sitcom full of blue-collar humor, and the world wondered who shot J.R. on *Dallas*. Movies ranged from *E.T.* to *Blade Runner* and theater audiences saw the first performances of the musical version of *Phantom of the Opera*.

In the doll world two distinct and popular dolls appeared. The Cabbage Patch doll caused a furor for the Christmas of 1983. People stood in line to buy the chubby toys and occasionally, when supplies ran short, fought over who was going to "adopt" them. A quieter emergence was appropriate for the American Girls made by Pleasant Company. Based on a philosophy that the dolls should educate as well as entertain girls, the American Girls came with a series of books that told the stories of the characters. Promoting positive values was a mission of the books and other product lines. The American Girls became a dominant force in the toy industry, although the dolls were in a niche for relatively affluent buyers.

Cabbage Patch Kids

DO YOU REMEMBER THE CABBAGE PATCH RIOTS? In Charleston, West Virginia, for example, five thousand shoppers rushed into a Hill's Department Store because each of them wanted at least one of the one hundred and twenty dolls inside. "They knocked over tables, fighting with each other," said the store's manager. "There were people in midair. It got ugly."

A woman suffered a broken leg and four others were injured when about one thousand people (some of whom had been waiting eight hours for the door to open) stormed into a Zayre department store in Wilkes-Barre, Pennsylvania. The store manager, who feared for his life, armed himself with a baseball bat.

These unbelievable scenes of chaos and violence were replayed throughout the country. And it was all because of the Cabbage Patch Kids.

The Cabbage Patch Kids actually began life about six years before their landmark mass-market introduction, when twenty-one-year-old Xavier Roberts, an art student, rediscovered an old German technique of fabric sculpture. He combined this technique with traditional Appalachian Mountain quilting skills to create pudgy baby dolls with homely, yet cute, facial expressions.

Roberts called his babies Little People, dressed them in baby clothes purchased at yard sales, and picked a name for each one from a 1937 baby book. Roberts's winning inspiration, however, was his marketing technique. He took the babies to arts and crafts shows around the Southeast and offered them for "adoption," complete with official "birth certificates."

Eager "parents" lined up to adopt the handmade Little People. After one little guy—Dexter—won first place at a craft show in Florida, Roberts had enough confidence to expand the concept. He organized five friends and incorporated Original Appalachian Artworks (O.A.A., Inc.).

Manny was made by Coleco in 1985. Like all Cabbage Patch Kids, he came with a tag with his name on it.

142

The first order of business for the new company was buying and renovating a former medical clinic in Cleveland, Georgia. The Neal Clinic, built in 1919, was transformed into BabyLand General Hospital, home of the Little People. BabyLand General has always been open to the public, and today it is one of the most popular tourist attractions in Georgia. BabyLand General is the home of Mother Cabbage and thus the birthplace of the Cabbage Patch Kids. Featured there is a display of early Little People.

In 1980 the Little People got national attention when they appeared on NBC's "Real People" television show. Over the next year, the babies were featured in the *Wall Street Journal*, *Newsweek*, and a host of other publications. People were crazy about Xavier Roberts's Little People. There were reports that early editions of the Little People were being "re-adopted" for up to one thousand dollars—twenty-five times the original adoption fee of forty dollars.

Two early editions especially worth noting are the signed, limited E Bronze Edition from late 1979 and the Grand Edition from the following year. Right after the E Bronze Edition was released, O.A.A. announced that most future editions would have stamped, screened, or embroidered signatures. Collectors predicted that the value of editions hand-signed by Roberts, such as the E Bronze, would skyrocket, and they did.

In 1982, O.A.A. negotiated a long-term licensing agreement with Coleco Industries to produce a baby with a vinyl head, a soft body, and an affordable price. O.A.A. changed the name of the Little People to the Cabbage Patch Kids, which could be registered and protected in all future product categories, and Mother Cabbage appeared at BabyLand General.

In 1983 Coleco Industries' Cabbage Patch Kids went on record as the most successful new dolls in the history of the toy industry. Almost three million Kids were delivered that year alone. Coleco stock jumped nineteen points in one day.

For the next three years, Cabbage Patch Kids were among the most popular dolls on the market. Coleco delivered mil-

Every Cabbage Patch Kid comes with adoption papers and a birth certificate.

Hope Azalia has a vinyl head and a cloth body and is sixteen inches tall like the other Coleco Cabbage Patch Kids.

Kirk Pierce is an original Appalachian Artworks cloth doll. Twenty-one inches tall, he has Xavier Roberts's signature on his shoe and his back.

lions of the licensed versions. In 1985, after a branch of BabyLand General opened on Fifth Avenue in Manhattan, more than a million people visited the Cabbage Patch and witnessed deliveries from a laboring Mother Cabbage.

Two years later Cabbage Patch Kids were the largest licensed property in the history of children's merchandising, with sales of more than four billion dollars. The following year, ten thousand people attended the first Easter Eggstravaganza at BabyLand General in Cleveland. By 1991 more than seventy-one million Cabbage Patch Kids had been adopted.

A change came in 1994, when O.A.A. licensed Mattel, the world's largest toy manufacturer, to produce and market Cabbage Patch Kids. The new line was introduced to great acclaim the following year. Mattel changed the packaging, updated the marketing plan, and created new designs; Cabbage Patch Kids were taking their second decade by storm!

These dolls made history again in 1992 when they were named the first and only official mascots of the U.S. Olympic Team. The Kids traveled with athletes to the Games in Barcelona, Spain, and made "Friends For Life" with patients in children's hospitals. In 1996, each member of the U.S. Olympic Team adopted his or her own Mattel OlympiKid before the Atlanta, Georgia, Games. The Cabbage Patch Kids were chosen as mascots because they "celebrate the individuality of the Team's athletes and exemplify camaraderie, sportsmanship, fair play, and dedication."

The Cabbage Patch in Cleveland has continued to deliver "hand-stitched-to-birth" original soft-sculpture Cabbage Patch Kids. More than six hundred and fifty thousand of these original babies have been adopted into homes around the world. Collectors even created the Xavier Roberts Collectors Club so they have a vehicle for learning more about the artist and discussing their soft-sculpture passion.

Although the hand-stitched, limited edition Cabbage Patch Kids go for hundreds of dollars, they are often spoken for even before they reach BabyLand General. In 1989, the entire edition of Bashful Billy, a hobo clown, was adopted before shipping began. In 1994, Baby Sidney, Baby Lanier, and the all-boy Cabbage Patch Kids Little People Edition were all adopted within days of delivery. The 1995 Christmas Edition, Treena, barely glimpsed the Official Adoption Centers nationwide before she was on her way home with her new parents.

Some said that the dolls were popular because they were something children could hold on to in a cold electronic age. Psychologists had numerous theories, suggesting that children identified with the dolls' not-so-beautiful looks; that the adoption papers echoed the fears and fantasies of many children; that the dolls made it possible for the children to feel like parents.

The children themselves, as always, got much nearer the mark. Asked why she liked her Cabbage Patch doll, one little girl answered matter-of-factly, "She has a real belly button."

Cabbage Patch Kids took the world by storm essentially because millions of people—children and adults—considered them cute and cuddly. Each was—and is—a bit different from the next (this is especially true of the hand-stitched originals). The adoption fee and birth certificate add a bit of ceremony to their acquisition, just like bringing home a real child.

And, after all, those outstretched arms just beg for hugs.

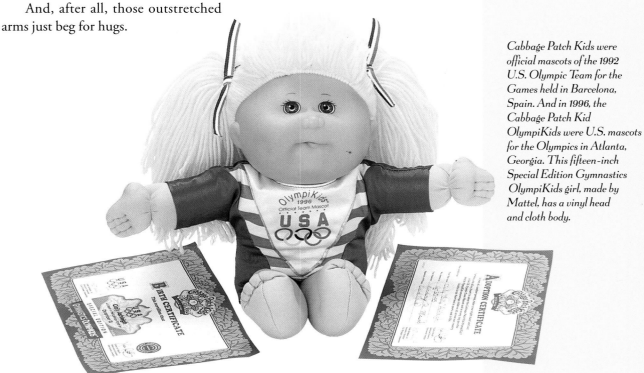

Cabbage Patch Kids were official mascots of the 1992 U.S. Olympic Team for the Games held in Barcelona, Spain. And in 1996, the Cabbage Patch Kid OlympiKids were U.S. mascots for the Olympics in Atlanta, Georgia. This fifteen-inch Special Edition Gymnastics OlympiKids girl, made by Mattel, has a vinyl head and cloth body.

The American Girl Dolls

GIRLS LOVE TO PLAY "LET'S PRETEND" WITH THEIR DOLLS. The doll can be a princess, a best friend, a baby, or even Laura Ingalls, depending on the day. Given a moment to arrange things, the bed is a jungle, a cotton swab is a magic wand, the doll is Girl Friday, and the heroine is off on another make-believe adventure.

Any girl will tell you that Let's Pretend is infinitely better with real props and costumes. Shoebox houses and old baby clothes are okay, but having the real goods—doll furniture, lots of clothes, and the germ of a story—takes Let's Pretend into another realm.

That's where Pleasant Company steps in. The company, founded in 1986 by Pleasant T. Rowland, an educator, creates books, dolls, clothing, accessories, and a magazine especially for girls. All the products are designed for fun, and they're also educational. According to Rowland, "We give girls chocolate cake with vitamins. Our books are exciting, our magazine is fun, and the dolls and accessories are pretty. But, most important, they give young girls a sense of self and an understanding of where they came from, and who they are today."

Pleasant Company's cornerstone is the American Girls Collection, which includes books, dolls, accessories, craft projects, and clothing based on five periods in American history. Each period is described through the adventures of an American Girl character: Felicity Merriman is a colonial girl growing up in Williamsburg, Virginia, in 1774; Kirsten Larson is a

Addy Walker is a courageous girl who lives in the time of the Civil War.

146

pioneer girl living on the frontier prairie in 1854; Addy Walker is determined to be free in 1864, during the Civil War; Samantha Parkington is a Victorian orphan living with her grandmother in 1904; and Molly McIntire is growing up during World War II in 1944.

Each character stars in a series of six books, which have such parallel themes as family, school, and holiday. By reading the books, girls make friends with the characters and learn how life in America has changed over the course of two hundred and twenty-five years. The historical aspects are emphasized in nonfiction picture essays at the end of each book.

Girls bring the books—and history— to life with the dolls and their accessories. Each eighteen-inch doll is made by Gotz in Germany and has posable vinyl arms, legs, and head; a soft cloth body; and eyes that open and close. Each character's hair is a different color, but it is always long enough to be styled into braids, curls, buns, or ponytails. Samantha, Kirsten, and Molly have bangs.

The dolls' clothes are historically accurate reproductions that match the book themes. Each doll has outfits, made from high-quality fabrics, for school, holiday, birthday, play, sleep, and other activities. Kirsten, for example, walks the traplines in a hand-knit woolen sweater, hat, and mittens. At Christmas, Molly wears a velvet dress and Felicity is resplendent in taffeta. Samantha goes to school in flannel. And

Orphaned Samantha Parkington, below left, lives with her wealthy grandmother in the turn-of-the-century Victorian era. Felicity Merriman is dressed like a typical girl in colonial Williamsburg in 1774.

The American Girl of Today collection is composed of twenty dolls who have a variety of hair and eye color and skin tones and are dressed in modern clothing.

Addy's work dress is sturdy cotton chambray. Even the shoes—from Felicity's buckled "single-last" shoes to Addy's cap-toed boots to Molly's oxfords—are period appropriate.

Like the clothing, all the accessories—and each doll has dozens—are historically accurate reproductions researched at historical societies and museums. Furniture like Kirsten's pine table and chairs, Samantha's brass-plated bed, and Addy's wooden school desk make girls wish that they, too, were eighteen inches tall. Other accessories include school equipment, toys, and dishes.

Most important to girls, however, is that the accessories "work." Addy's ice-cream freezer, Felicity's tea-cakes kit, and Samantha's paint set are designed to involve projects for girls to do with their dolls. The furniture drawers open and doors shut, beds have blankets, and dishes come with tiny "food." Samantha's whistle blows and her flower press presses; Molly's tiny snow dome actually works, as does Addy's abacus.

Pleasant Company has also created cookbooks, craft books, theater kits, and paper dolls that explain historic pastimes so girls can immerse themselves in the occupations of yesteryear. Other complementary products include trading cards, buttons, posters, bookmarks, balloons, and, for the truly ambitious, dress patterns so young seamstresses can make their dolls' clothes.

A girl chooses her doll based on how she looks, her clothing and accessories, and her stories. Be that as it may, the company has so far sold more Samanthas than all the other four dolls. There are, however, some interesting patterns in the way people purchase the dolls: Kirsten tends to be very popular in Minnesota and the Midwest. Molly is often popular with adults because many people recall growing up during the '40s and can relate to Molly's stories about America during World War II.

Although some adults are buying the American Girl dolls for their own collections, the dolls were not conceived and are not marketed as collector's items, and are not produced in limited editions.

Pleasant Company recently introduced a new collection for girls who are curious about their place in today's world. The American Girl of Today collection includes twenty dolls with a variety of features. The doll can be chosen by skin tone, hair color, and eye color so that she represents the individuality of her owner. Like the American Girls Collection, American Girl of Today dolls are eighteen inches tall and have vinyl limbs and heads, sleep eyes, and cloth bodies. They wear such modern outfits as leggings, jeans, T-shirts, baseball caps, and hair scrunchies.

The accessories are more modern, too. They include a library card, lunch ticket, "dollar" bills, a working calculator, a sleeping bag, and bunk beds. The Girl of Today can cuddle her own six-inch American Girl doll, or she might prefer a tiny teddy bear.

Like the historical dolls, each American Girl of Today comes with books. Rather than telling the doll's story, however, the books are blank and invite girls to write their own stories, either about their dolls or about themselves.

This eighteen-inch American Girl of Today has blond hair and blue eyes. She is holding her six-inch Felicity.

The American Girls of Today have a great variety of outfits and accessories suitable for all occasions.

American Girl Gear, the American Girl Library, and *American Girl* magazine round out the American Girl of Today collection. Girl Gear is a collection of child-sized versions of the doll accessories: a sleeping bag, nightshirt, hat, vest, watch, and book bag, for example. The Library is composed of five books especially for girls—advice, games, a diary-scrapbook, a birthday card kit, and crafts. Many of the ideas in the book are based on *American Girl* magazine, also published by Pleasant Company.

Pleasant Company's American Girls and American Girl of Today collections are intended for girls from the ages seven to twelve. And although Pleasant Company is "very committed" to elementary-age girls, the company recently introduced a collection that reaches back to younger girls, ages three and up.

Bitty Baby is a fifteen-inch baby doll with a soft cloth body, arms, legs, and head of vinyl, painted or molded hair, and sleep eyes. There are four Bitty Baby ethnicities: African American, Asian American, Caucasian, and Hispanic. Each Bitty Baby comes with her own Bitty Bear, a five-inch teddy bear with posable arms and legs.

Bitty Baby is available in four ethnicities— African American, Asian American, Caucasian, and Hispanic. Each baby comes with a little Bitty Bear.

As with all Pleasant Company's product lines, Bitty Baby's collection is centered on a series of books with seasonal and family themes. Bitty Bear stars in the board books and coloring books that teach young children about daily activities like dressing, meals, and bedtime.

Like her older sisters, Bitty Baby has a wide variety of clothing. Each outfit comes with the appropriate book and includes coordinating clothes for Bitty Bear. Besides her dresses, sweater, Halloween costume, and playsuit, Bitty Baby has such accessories as a booster chair, dishes, pretend food, a wagon, a baby carrier, and a diaper-bag set.

Acknowledgments

WE WOULD LIKE TO RECOGNIZE AND THANK the following people whose often pioneering research, writings, and occasionally personal guidance were the chief sources of information contained in these pages:

John Axe, Ann Bahar, Karen Bender, Loraine Burdick, Diana Serra Cary, Barbara Lutz Comienski, Gary Coville, Virginia Davis, Jan Foulke, Patikii and Tyson Gibbs, Susan Girardot, Mary Gorham, Barbara Guyette, Virginia Heyerdahl, Judith Izen, Don Jensen, Pam and Polly Judd, Katherine Kuckens, Jan Lebow, Kim Rose Lusk, A. Glenn Mandeville, Laura Meisner, Ursula R. Mertz, Peggy Millhose, Donna Miska, Jeanne Niswonger, Edward R. Pardella, Vincent Santelmo, Patricia N. Schoonmaker, Mary Rickert Stuecher, Deborah Thompson, Anne Votaw, Jacqueline Wilson, and Diane Goff Yupatoff.

We especially want to thank our friends who so kindly allowed us to photograph dolls from their prized collections:

Minnie Baker, Helen Bernat, Barbara Brown, Patricia A. Brown, Janet Clendenien, John Clendenien, Carolyn Cook, Laura Cook, Marcellene Currens, Margaret Dowling, Betty Ebaugh, Kathy Evans, Mary Fox, Virginia Ann Heyerdahl, Lamont Mahoney, Terry Mahoney, Eleanor Mauck, Lindsay Mauck, Richard Mauck, Emily Reitz, Lovena Smith, Diane Sutton, Deborah Thompson, Rosalie Thompson, Jennifer Weber, Amy Wood, and Gladys Woodward.

We also want to thank our friends for the use of photographs from their personal archives:

John Axe, Beth Gunther, Judith Izen, Polly Judd, and Cris Johnson.

The publisher is grateful to Pleasant Company for the use of its photographs. The American Girls Collection, Bitty Baby Collection, American Girl of Today and *American Girl* magazine are trademarks of Pleasant Company.